THE WONDERS
OF THE WORLD

IRENA TREVISAN

THE WONDERS
OF THE WORLD

Translated by
SALLYANN DELVINO

CHARTWELL
BOOKS

P. 2: THE PROFILE OF THE SPHINX IS ONE
OF THE MOST EMBLEMATIC SYMBOLS OF THE
WONDERS OF THE ANCIENT WORLD.
PP. 4-5: VIEW OF THE TAJ MAHAL AND
REFLECTING POOL. THE FRONTAL PERSPECTIVE
EPITOMIZES A SENSE OF SYMMETRY, AND
THE REFLECTION OF THE DOME IN THE POOL
AMPLIFIES ITS GRANDEUR.
PP. 6-7: THE UNIQUENESS OF THE XI'AN
TERRACOTTA ARMY LIES IN THE INCREDIBLE
DETAILED REALISM OF THE FACES, ARMOR,
AND GESTURES, EVOKING THE CAPTIVATING
SENSATION OF STANDING BEFORE A GENUINE
ARMY, READY TO DEFEND THE EMPEROR QIN
SHI HUANG DI.
PP. 8-9: THE WHITE PLASTER VOLUTES
AND MIRROR DECORATION OF THE WAT
RONG KHUN TEMPLE IN THAILAND CREATE
DAZZLING AND EVOCATIVE REFLECTIONS WITH
THE SUNLIGHT.
OPPOSITE: THE PYRAMIDS OF KHUFU,
KHAFRE, AND MENKAURE STAND OUT ON THE
GIZA PLAIN, AT THE PERIPHERY OF CAIRO.

Opposite: The enchanting Iguaçu
waterfalls, on the border between
Argentina and Brazil, form the heart
of a lush and flourishing ecosystem of
extraordinary biodiversity.
Pp. 14-15: *Mano del Desierto* (*Hand
of the Desert*), by Chilean artist
Mario Irarrázabal, seems to rise
directly from the subsoil of the
Atacama Desert, solitary and silent.
Pp. 16-17: Marvelous works of
human ingenuity, the cathedral and
the famous leaning tower stand
elegantly on the green of Pisa's
Piazza dei Miracoli.

Contents

Pp. 18-19: The snow-capped peak of Mount Fuji, framed by cherry trees in bloom.
Pp. 20-21: The portraits of the four American presidents seem to emerge naturally from the rock of Mount Rushmore, a granite massif in the Black Hills.
Opposite: The white expanse of the Uyuni salt flats, in Bolivia, merges with the sky at the horizon.

INTRODUCTION

It seems almost impossible to embrace in a single, immediate vision the enormous architectural, monumental, artistic, and natural heritage of our planet. The great diffusion of collections and compendia that over the centuries have attempted to organize in precise lists the immense number of *wonders* of the known world embodies the challenge of creating such a universal summation and, at the same time, offers a testament to the eternal interest and timeless curiosity of human beings before the extraordinary, the majestic, and the incredible.

The complexity of the collections dedicated to this subject reflects the semantic diversity of the word itself, *wonder*, that which evokes a sentiment of immediate and fleeting aesthetic amazement—therefore different from admiration—affecting both senses and spirit. For the Ancients, authors of the first wonders of the world, this amazement was not necessarily connected to beauty, as modern vocabulary would warrant in the majority of cases. *Stupor mundi* created, for the first thinkers, the foundation of philosophical reflection, enriched by a sacral component: wonder before the world and its phenomena—terrifying because unknown—motivates questioning and reflection, the quintessential endeavors of the human mind. The ethical and aesthetic spheres end up, theoretically, separating from one another.

It is undeniable, however, in the face of the first list of the *thaumata* ("wonders") dating to the second century BC, the beauty of the works listed is not irrelevant. The Pyramids of Giza, Hanging Gardens of Babylon, Colossus of Rhodes, Statue of Zeus at Olympia, Temple of Artemis at Ephesus, Mausoleum at Halicarnassus, and Lighthouse of Alexandria are seven monuments of culture the magnificence of which is nearly matched by their aesthetic splendor, the harmony of form and majestic charm only enriching the significance of these monuments that emerge prominently as genuine icons of ages, characters, and civilizations of the past. The wonder thus comes into being, for the amazement they

arouse and for the cultural story to which they allude, a *monumentum*: an emblematic work of aspiration from its own era, a memorial that persists through time for its artistic, symbolic, and cultural value. It is now second nature to associate the Pyramids of Giza with the Ancient Egyptian civilization, to identify Ancient Rome with the Colosseum, Classical Greece with the Parthenon, the Maya with Chichén Itzá: in originality and conceptual content, these testimonies have assumed a far-reaching symbolic value more than other expressions of human ingenuity.

From the earliest collections of the Hellenistic period, which satisfied the stylized characteristics of the time and, in the same breath, a curiosity before an Alexandrian world of broadening borders and diminishing limits, interest in *wonders* bourgeoned at nearly a constant pace. From the Latin authors—Vitruvius, Pliny the Elder, Seneca—to the *De septem orbis spectaculis* of the fifth century AD until the Renaissance, the fascination of great works of human creativity and ingenuity does not cease to speak. In the lists inherited through the centuries, however, the limits of the past are immediately apparent and contingent. Scarcer knowledge in the past of the surrounding world proved substantively restricting. Moreover, within an already limited known reality, approach and exploration was further restricted, favoring at times canon over science. The number *seven* of the wonders of the world, maintained for centuries, is not coincidental: seven are the sages of Ancient Greece, the kings of Rome, and the plagues of Egypt, continuing transversally across different civilizations and epochs. The subsequent expansion of the geographic horizon and the development in scientific thought have naturally multiplied, to this day, the possibilities of choice.

As we cross the threshold of the third millennium, it becomes indispensable to raise our gaze to the broader horizon. Unraveled from reverential trepidation and replaced by deep respect for the captivating

achievements of human ingenuity and majestic expressions of nature—and by the ambition to create a unique and disciplined collection—the reverent sense of astonishment prevails today before these incredible works of beauty. The modern approach branches outward, therefore, to discover masterpieces of art and architecture both ancient and modern (Angkor Wat, Taj Mahal, Sydney Opera House), primordial emblems that touch legend and myth (the Moai, Stonehenge, Machu Picchu), singular symbols standing watch over our modern cities (Eiffel Tower, Statue of Liberty, Christ the Redeemer), human-made natural sites (rice terraces of China, salt flats of Lanzarote), and amazing phenomena of indomitable

forces of nature (Victoria Falls, Mount Etna, Perito Moreno Glacier). The categories compound and interweave within a modern perspective, distinctive of interactivity, denoting *wonder* in all its forms and valences. The modern result, more than a finite compendium, is a perpetual exploration of the world's macroscopic expressions of the beautiful.

Within this undetermined expansion, the modern world is increasingly focused on precise legislation, a result of the growing desire to safeguard the expressions of our heritage, the resoundingly self-evident as well as the more delicate and subtle of our legacies. The ten criteria established by UNESCO to define the wonders of the world today—beside designating masterpieces

of exceptional beauty of human creative ingenuity and of phenomena by nature—endeavor to identify and protect crucial habitats for the conservation of diversity and areas under threat that hold particular scientific and ecological importance. The lengthy list of UNESCO World Heritage Sites—currently more than one thousand entries—should be read with a far-reaching perspective, progressively more important, to the preservation and valorization of those works of beauty that in the globalized world are perennially reachable but also potentially at risk.

Before such a rich and varied subject (principally geographical and temporal), to sum up the significance of an additional collection is immaterial and subjective.

Only by keeping alive that primary feeling, the *fil rouge* of this genre of exploration, is it possible to untangle within this crowded list the beautiful natural and human-created phenomena of the planet: we once more retrieve the pure and simple sense of *wonder* in the presence of that which amazes, captivates, and intrigues. Beauty can therefore serve as the vehicle for a deeper respect of the world and of the achievements in human history: the natural phenomena and human-created wonders to be protected from our own destructive forces. As Sophocles wrote, "Many are the wondrous things, but no more wondrous than man."

To be included in UNESCO's World Heritage List, a site must meet one or more of the following ten criteria:

1. Represent a masterpiece of human creative genius.
2. Exhibit an interchange of cultural value within a period of time in the field of archaeology, architecture, or technology, artistic or environmental.
3. Bear a unique or exceptional testimony to a cultural tradition or civilization.
4. Offer an outstanding example of a type of architectural, technological, or environmental construction that illustrates a significant stage in human history.
5. Be an outstanding example of human interaction with the environment.
6. Be directly associated to events connected with ideas, beliefs, traditions, or artistic and literary works of exceptional universal significance.
7. Represent natural phenomena or areas of exceptional natural beauty and aesthetic importance.
8. Be an outstanding representative example of major epochs of earth's history that bear testimony to life or geological processes.
9. Be an outstanding example of ecological and biological processes in the evolution of the ecosystem.
10. Contain a natural habitat most representative and important for the conservation of biodiversity, including threatened areas having a particular exceptional value from the point of view of science or conservation.

WONDERS OF THE ANCIENT WORLD

Turning our gaze to the wonders of the ancient world, it would be impossible to exclude the canonical list of the seven works of extraordinary beauty from the Hellenistic Period. The richness of this subject, documented by a vast bibliography distributed across more than two thousand years of history, finds its unique starting point with this first list, discovered in Alexandria, from the second century BC: the canonical Epigram of Antipater of Sidon, preserved in the *Palatine Anthology*. The first drafting of the list of the seven wonders of the world deeply and broadly reflects the cultural reality of the time. Following the conquests of Alexander the Great, which had sanctioned the birth of a great Macedonian-Greek empire, opportunity bourgeoned for exploring beyond the cultural *koiné*, driving a sense of intellectual curiosity toward the surrounding lands. The perception of diversity in encountering the remains of former great empires—mighty pharaonic Egypt, glorious ancient Babylon—offered new and distinct opportunity for the recognition and admiration of captivating masterpieces of extraordinary beauty, echoes of the *megaloprépeia* (magnificence) of sovereigns, legendary figures, and mythical beings of a past that already, in some cases, seemed remote. To this we add the birth of a new approach to written text and research, conceiving the construction of the great library of Alexandria, to classify and compare the enormous, heterogeneous corpus of literature, organized in the structures of indexes, lists, glossaries, and catalogs: a literary genre that grew prolifically to collect and parse in patterns and numbers impressions relating to the surrounding world.

The gaze of the Alexandrians on these beautiful masterpieces would have been undeniably privileged. Before the destruction of these structures (all except the Giza pyramids, which remain intact), the seven wonders of the ancient world were contemporaneously visible for only thirty years in the second half of the third century: a brief time when a traveler could admire the captivating masterpieces of human creative power and ability without straying too far from the *mare nostrom*. Departing from Greece, the traveler could genuflect

before the awe-inspiring simulacrum of Zeus, forged by the talent of Phidias, in the temple of Olympia; pass through the port of Rhodes to gaze upon the colossus of the patron god, Helios, guarding the ships; head east to reach the great Ephesus and its *Artemision*, with columns decorated in relief; continue on to Halicarnassus to admire the polychrome temple dedicated to king Mausolus; travel to the East and the ancient legends of Babylon, with its walls and lavish gardens; return to the gates of the Mediterranean to arrive at the splendid Lighthouse of Alexandria, standing vigil over the city; and, finally, stand at the foot of the great pyramids of the Giza plain, captivating by their sharp geometric lines and harmoniously intrinsic to the desert landscape. In a rather limited circumnavigation, a traveler could touch the very works that have sown the inception of architectural achievements for two millennia, serving both formal inspiration and reference by their powerful symbolism, visual impact, harmony with the surrounding natural scenery, and representative force of their forms.

In a modern collection of wonders of the ancient world still visible today, we cannot ignore the great lessons of the past. With only one *wonder* still extant from the canonical set (the Great Pyramid of Giza), an ideal journey into formidable ancient works of captivating beauty that remain in our modern day inevitably broadens the horizon from the classical land of the Mediterranean to the whole of the world.

The great pyramid of Khufu remains an iconic symbol of the wonders in human history: a gigantic monument in stone, more than seven hundred feet high, rising majestically to testify to the great empire that emerged on the banks of the Nile nearly five thousand years before the birth of Christ. From the initial accounts of travelers and scholars of Greek culture and language who visited the vestiges of Ancient Egypt before the arrival of Christianity to the research of antiquarians and eighteenth-century scientists following Napoleon's expedition and to the modern-day voyages on the Nile organized by official travel agencies, the pyramids of Giza have been a fulcrum of archaeological interest and

a symbol of fascination inherited from the past. Passing from Egyptian to classical architecture, we note an evolution of intent in which monumental achievements veer from the celebration of absolute power (worldly and otherworldly) to inspiration founded more on function, operating for collective and communal ends: the Parthenon, great wonder of Greece, dedicated to the divinity and a vital center of the *polis*, where religion and sociality work in tandem. The extraordinary harmony of the Parthenon's classical lines and ornament, set within the natural context above, in symbolic dominion over the city, is not only emblematic of Athenian democracy but also one of the purest artistic expressions of incomparable beauty belonging to human history. The temple of the Doric order, with its continuous Ionic frieze that would have measured 525 feet long, its free-standing statues in the pediment, and its 92 metopes carved by Phidias would have housed the monumental chryselephantine statue of Athena *Parthenos*, a feminine equivalent of the famous effigy of Zeus at the temple of Olympia, recorded in the canonical list of wonders of the ancient world.

The social aspect of classical architecture becomes even stronger in the Roman world. It is impossible not to think of the massive crowds besieging the Colosseum to watch the spectacle of gladiators, athletes, and exotic animals, making the arcades of the most famous monument of Ancient Rome tremble. Since 1980, the UNESCO World Heritage List has included the Flavian Amphitheater as one of the new seven wonders of the world, a list determined by a referendum organized by the New Open World Corporation. Symbol of the Roman Empire, the very heart of Rome, and the whole

of Italy, the Colosseum knows unprecedented world renown. Beyond the most iconic expressions, canons of classical architecture are diffuse throughout the Old World, offering its timeless wonders: from the frigid lands of Britannia, where the imposing Hadrian's Wall emerges, to the warm Turkish coasts, where the sun shines on the tall columns of the Library of Celsus, then descending toward the Arabian Peninsula and the surreal architectural structures of Petra in the heart of the desert, Hellenistic forms emerging from yellow-ochre rock. To choose from among these stunning works proves an arduous task, as every corner of the Mediterranean offers awe-inspiring sites, where formal styles and inspirations blend in the creations of spectacular beauty.

The great privilege of modernity is the ability to look beyond the limits of classical civilization. In a contemporary compilation, attention must be paid to Antiquity across its most diverse expressions, echoes of other magnificent and ancient civilizations, in some cases buried by time, nature, or neglect. And here, as we move toward the East, we come into contact with ancient empires, dynasties, and kingdoms of rare majesty, with the most striking architectural expressions of these complex societies, characterized by a centralization of power symbolically represented, expressions of its legitimacy. The unmistakable protagonist of China was born in this way and with it, the Great Wall: the result of a functional intent (defense) expresses in concrete form the far-reaching vastness of the Chinese Empire and of those who ruled it. Almost 5,500 miles long, the Wall is the insignia the ancient Chinese civilization sought to leave upon a land to claim eternal possession of it. Today

it is difficult to look at the remaining sections of the wall without an overwhelming sense of reverential awe. The greatness of the Chinese Empire came also to be sought in other macroscopic forms, unique in the world, such as the incredible rows of terracotta faces belonging to the legendary Xi'an Army or the splendid lines of the Forbidden City in Beijing, which evoke a fascinating history intertwined with legend. The mythical past of the East has many expressions: impossible to ignore is the linear architecture of Japan, with creations that reflect profound philosophical and religious speculation, intrinsic to the austerity of its essential forms, in harmony with the natural balance. Among the many, the Otowa-san Kiyomizu-dera temple in Kyoto exemplifies dry formal inspiration rich in the poetry of Japanese art (free of the baroque elements of the Chinese opulence), constructed without nails and in organic contact with the surrounding nature, dominated by green hills and a picturesque waterfall (from which the temple takes its name). Of an entirely different nature, the mausoleum of Angkor Wat, in Cambodia, is an immense temple-mountain bounded by a moat, an expression of the architecture of the Khmer: imposing ogival towers (in the form of lotus buds), terraces, corridors, narratives in bas-relief, gilded stucco, and statues of great dimension express an Asian wonder characteristic of the southeast, tied inextricably to the divine and in close dialogue with a flora at times invasive, encompassing the architecture that seems to rise from the forest itself.

On an ideal journey among the wonders of Antiquity, the mind travels agilely to the New World, long unknown, where other great empires prospered before the arrival of the Europeans, with unprecedented architecture, fascinating and enwrapped in legend. It is here we admire the mammoth Kukulkan pyramid in Chichén Itzá of the Maya, part of an archaeological complex that had once been an important Mayan city: a temple dedicated to Quetzalcoatl, the imposing construction serves as a symbol of the great reverence of the Mesoamerican people before the divine and its expressions. The height of the complex stretches to the sky and its form ensures contact with the supernatural: along the north stairway, during the spring and the autumn equinox, the corners of the pyramid project a shadow in the shape of a feathered snake, symbol of the god. The wonder of a construction is even further accentuated by natural context in the Inca city of Machu Picchu, built on terraces set in the Peruvian Andes, surrounded in rain and Amazon forest populated by endangered species, engendering to the human ruins the unique and timeless fascination of the Lost World civilizations.

It would be impossible to conclude this ideal journey without a leap into the depths of legend, in which unassuming Easter Island hides a true gem of the past. Lost in the Pacific, far from everything and everyone, the famous Moai emerge alone to guard the island: sculpted in dark basaltic tufa and bearing mysterious *rongorongo* glyphs, these deified ancestors contemplate their land with a stalwart and solemn regard, the keepers of an ancient and marvelous history.

PYRAMIDS OF GIZA

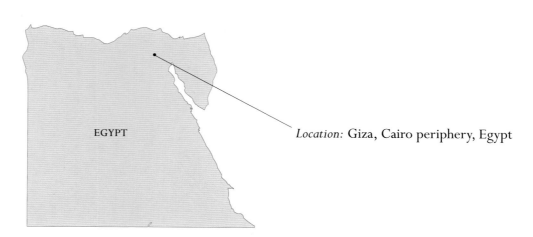

EGYPT

Location: Giza, Cairo periphery, Egypt

The three pyramids of Giza are perhaps the emblem of all the wonders of the world, for their longevity, cultural relevance, uniqueness, and fame. No other symbol better identifies Ancient Egypt than the funerary pyramid structures that emerge alongside what was the capital of the Old Kingdom: Memphis. The Great Pyramid of Khufu marks one of the original *wonders* listed in the first compendium of *seven wonders* by Antipater of Sidon during the Hellenistic Period; the only surviving from the original canon, the Great Pyramid endured for approximately four thousand years as the tallest structure ever built by humankind. The construction consists of 2 million blocks of stone, limestone from Aswan for the outer casing and granite from Tura for the king's chamber and monoliths of the interior, reaching an amassed weight of approximately 7 million tons. The construction took over twenty years, requiring architects, craftsmen, artisans, and slaves, all serving the almighty pharaoh. Still, after four millennia, fascination for the pyramid of Khufu inspires scientific and archaeological exploration, which has led, even most recently, to the discovery of hidden spaces within.

OPPOSITE: SPHINX OF GIZA. IN THE BACKGROUND, THE PYRAMID OF KHAFRE, THE ONLY PYRAMID THAT RETAINS A PART OF THE WHITE LIMESTONE (OF TURA) THAT ORIGINALLY COVERED THE ENTIRE STRUCTURE. BELOW: VIEW OF THE THREE GREAT PYRAMIDS SET IN THE LANDSCAPE OF THE DESERT TERRAIN.

Date: XXV century BC

Definition: Royal necropolis comprising the three pyramids dedicated to the pharaohs Khufu, Khafre, and Menkaure.

Dimensions of the Great Pyramid: Base side length 755 feet, height 480.6 feet (today, 453 feet), surface area 12 acres.

State of preservation: The limestone outer casing is lost; the structures are subject to heavy erosion.

Acknowledgments: The Great Pyramid of Khufu is the only remaining of the original seven wonders of the ancient world. The necropolis has been listed a UNESCO World Heritage Site since 1979.

STONEHENGE

Location: Near Amesbury, Wiltshire, England

ENGLAND

Erected as sentinels in Salisbury Plain, the megaliths of Stonehenge have for centuries held a profound fascination. The basic structure consists of a large stone circle, 108 feet in diameter, originally constructed of thirty stones, of which seventeen have survived. Originally, this was probably a construction in wood, replaced by stone around 2500 BC, following a precise alignment. The axis of Stonehenge, in fact, is aligned according to the position of the sun at dawn during the summer solstice, giving rise to numerous theories about the monument's functional, ritual, and astronomical significance. Recent excavations have proved that the site had served as a burial place. Stonehenge is the most famous Neolithic site in the world.

OPPOSITE: STONEHENGE, CONSISTING OF MEGALITHS ARRANGED IN A CIRCLE. BELOW: THE STONEHENGE MEGALITHS WERE RESTORED TO THEIR ORIGINAL POSITION DURING RECONSTRUCTION WORK IN THE EARLY-TWENTIETH CENTURY: THEIR ALIGNMENT AROUSES CURIOSITY AND DEBATE.

Date: 3000 BC–2500 BC

Definition: Neolithic site comprising a series of megaliths arranged in a circle and aligned to the position of the sun.

Dimensions: Diameter 108 feet.

State of preservation: Good; the site was restored in the first half of the twentieth century, however is jeopardized by traffic pollution and congestion from the nearby motorway.

Acknowledgments: UNESCO World Heritage Site since 1986.

PETRA

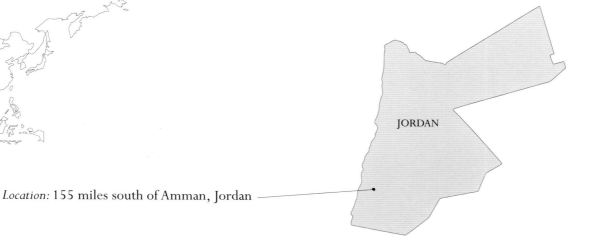

JORDAN

Location: 155 miles south of Amman, Jordan

"Petra is the most wonderful place in the world, not for the sake of its ruins, which are quite a secondary affair, but for the colour of its rocks, all red and black and gray with streaks of green and blue…so you will never know what Petra is like, unless you come out here…" Thus Lawrence of Arabia described the "pink city" heart of Jordan, capital of the Nabataeans and market town of strategic importance in the extensive commercial network of trade between the Mediterranean and the East. The exquisite beauty of the site derives from the combination of the structures and the sandstone in which they are hewn, rich in spectacular color variation and in lines of Hellenistic inspiration. Much of the fascination of Petra lies within the depths of a narrow desert gorge, between rock walls and mountains set against the open sky, where there is but little distinction between natural and human construction. Petra's designation in 2007 as one of the new seven wonders of the world brought many more visitors to the area.

OPPOSITE: THE MONUMENTAL FAÇADE OF THE ARCHAEOLOGICAL SITE OF PETRA, IN JORDAN, KNOWN AS *EL KHASNEH* ("THE TREASURE"). FROM THE NARROW GORGE THAT GIVES ACCESS TO THE AREA, THE VIEW SUDDENLY OPENS ONTO THIS INCREDIBLE ARCHITECTURE CARVED INTO THE ROCK.
BELOW: DETAILS OF THE ROYAL TOMBS OF PETRA: TO THE LEFT, THE PALACE TOMB AND CORINTHIAN TOMB.
PP. 42-43: VIEW OF THE *MONASTERY* (*AL-DEIR*) OF PETRA, INITIALLY INTENDED FOR THE SEPULCHER OF KING OBODAS I, LATER USED AS A PLACE OF WORSHIP DURING THE BYZANTINE ERA.

Date: Edomite settlement from the VII century BC; Nabataean city from the VI century BC; period of greatest prosperity around the middle of the I century AD.

Definition: Nabataean capital established at an important commercial nexus between the East and West, at the crossroads of a caravan road on the Incense Route.

Dimensions: Approximately 37 square miles.

State of preservation: Good. Discovered in 1812 by Johann Ludwig Burckhardt; still under archaeological study.

Acknowledgments: UNESCO World Heritage Site since 1985; listed as one of the new seven wonders of the world.

THE PARTHENON

Location: Acropolis of Athens, Greece

GREECE

No other monument better symbolizes the beauty of Classical Greece. The harmony of the Doric forms, which stand against the sky on top of the Acropolis hill, echoes the grandeur of the fifth century, the era of Pericles, Sophocles, Zeno, and, in the arts, the sculptor Phidias. Phidias, with the architects Ictinus, Callicrates, and Mnesikles, gave form and life to the magnificent temple dedicated to Athena. Constructed with marble from Mount Pentelicus with funds from the treasure of the Delian League, the temple stood vigil over the city of Athens, its structures and forms exemplifying the Golden Ratio (identified by Pythagoras in the previous century). Of awe-inspiring beauty are the metopes, Ionic frieze, and pediments, while the vision of the chryselephantine statue of the goddess within, Phidias's masterpiece now lost, would have been breathtaking.

OPPOSITE: FRONTAL VIEW OF THE PARTHENON, CONSTRUCTED TO REPLACE THE EARLIER TEMPLE OF ATHENA *POLIÀS* DESTROYED BY THE PERSIANS IN 480 BC. BELOW: THE PARTHENON OVERLOOKS THE CITY OF ATHENS FROM THE ACROPOLIS.

Date: V century BC

Definition: Doric peripteral temple dedicated to the goddess Athena *Parthenos.*

Dimensions: 228 x 101 feet, column height 34.3 feet (with frieze and pediment, approximately 43 feet).

State of preservation: In 1687 the Parthenon was used as a gunpowder storehouse by the Ottomans, and a Venetian cannon ball destroyed a good part of the structure. In 1801 Count Elgin transported numerous marbles to England, depriving the temple of its sculptures, still housed at the British Museum. During the war against the Turks, the Turkish forces demolished numerous columns to extract metal for bullets. The state of preservation is therefore not good, with a UNESCO-funded restoration project in progress.

Acknowledgments: UNESCO World Heritage Site since 1987.

GREAT WALL OF CHINA

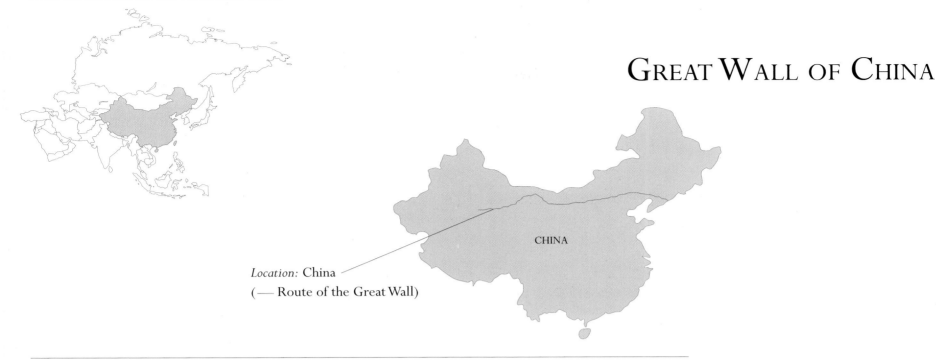

CHINA

Location: China
(— Route of the Great Wall)

Built by countless workers under the Qin dynasty, the Great Wall of China is the most imposing human construction of Antiquity. It is estimated that during its construction, 400,000 laborers perished, a misfortune that, at a time, ascribed to the wall the epithet "the longest cemetery in the world." The first sections of the wall were constructed using a wooden frame filled with a simple mix of earth and gravel. The fortified walls and sight towers that remain today were built at a later date, under the Ming Dynasty (1338–1644), using local stone and brickwork. The structure, between approximately 23 and 26 feet high and 18 and 21 feet wide, supported a pathway on the top of the wall that served as a means of communication in times of peril. From the lookout towers, danger was signaled by a series of fires lit in sequence. The imposing grandeur of the Great Wall is undeniable: in the heart of China it traverses ten provinces (Qinghai, Gansu, Ningxia, Shaanxi, Inner Mongolia, Hebei, …). The only truly protected section is located north of Beijing, close to the city, while other less visited sections are, unfortunately, at risk of erosion.

OPPOSITE: SECTION OF THE GREAT WALL WITH WATCHTOWERS PLACED AT REGULAR INTERVALS TO ALLOW VISUAL COMMUNICATION BETWEEN THE SOLDIERS, BY MEANS OF A SYSTEM OF FLAGS BY DAY AND OF FIRES BY NIGHT.
BELOW AND PP. 48-49: THE ROUTE OF THE GREAT WALL TRACES THE PHYSICAL GEOGRAPHY OF THE CHINESE TERRITORY.

Date: III century BC

Definition: Long series of defensive walls constructed to protect against invasions by neighboring peoples.

Length: 5,500 miles.

State of preservation: Many sections of the wall are in ruins and subject to vandalism; the wall is also at risk from heavy rains and sand storms, pollution, and mass tourism.

Acknowledgments: UNESCO World Heritage Site since 1987; listed one of the new seven wonders of the world.

THE TERRACOTTA ARMY

CHINA

Location: Lintong, near the city of Xi'an, Shaanxi Province, China

In March 1974 a Chinese farmer, digging a well, by chance unearthed a number of pits containing terracotta statues, vases, and utensils. It was the beginning of one of the most striking archaeological discoveries of the last century: under a mound of more than 165 feet lay the cavernous mausoleum of emperor Qin Shi Huang, founder of the first unified empire in Chinese history. The funerary room has walls in bronze and contains a life-size army in terracotta, platoons of soldiers carved with detailed accuracy: infantry, archers, halberdiers, and horses depicted in extraordinary realism to faithfully represent in facial characteristic and measure the army that had united China. Estimated to contain from 6,000 to 8,000 artifacts, of which only a small portion has come to light, this archaeological site has more to reveal still.

Date: 260–210 BC

Definition: Life-size reproduction in terracotta of the emperor's army in the tomb of the first Chinese emperor Qin Shi Huang.

Dimensions: The archaeological site covers an area of 21.72 square miles.

State of preservation: Very good; discovered by chance in 1974, the site has remained intact for centuries.

Acknowledgments: UNESCO World Heritage Site since 1987.

OPPOSITE: EACH WARRIOR POSSESSES HIS OWN PHYSIOGNOMY AND PARTICULAR TRAITS DEPICTED IN STRIKING REALISM: THE DETAILS OF THE ARMOR AND THE POSITIONS OF THE BODY AND HANDS PROVIDE INFORMATION ABOUT THE COMBAT TECHNIQUES OF THE INFANTRY, HALBERDIERS, ARCHERS, AND ARBALISTS. PP. 54-55: THE TERRACOTTA ARMY IS LOCATED IN EIGHT EXCAVATED PITS ONE AND HALF MILES WEST OF THE IMPERIAL TOMB. THE PRINCIPAL CORPS ENCOMPASSES APPROXIMATELY 6,000 WARRIORS AND TWO CHARIOTS OF WAR.

THE COLOSSEUM

ITALY

Location: Rome, Italy

Symbol of ancient Rome, the great amphitheater built under the Flavian dynasty is one of the most impressive and significant monuments of classical antiquity. Constructed not far from the Roman Forum, the Colosseum has for centuries served the heart of the city of Rome and its social life. The structure expresses the highest standards of architecture from the Imperial Era, exemplified in the use of the arches and vaults and convex elliptical perimeter. Spectacles of gladiator fighting, extravagant hunts, dramatic performances, and battle re-enactments took place within the Colosseum walls: audience capacity could reach between 50,000 and 75,000 spectators. Under the floor of the arena, covered with sand, wound an intricate maze of service rooms, animal cages, armories, hoists, and complex machinery for *special effects*.

OPPOSITE: VIEW OF THE COLOSSEUM FROM VIA DEI FORI IMPERIALI.
BELOW: INSIDE THE FLAVIAN AMPHITHEATER, THE CENTRAL AREA DEDICATED TO THE SPECTACLES, NOW MISSING ITS FLOOR, REVEALS THE SERVICE AREAS BENEATH THAT HOUSED THE ARENA'S STORAGE ROOMS, ANIMAL CAGES, AND CELLS FOR THE SLAVES AND GLADIATORS.
PP. 58-59: SUGGESTIVE OVERVIEW OF THE THREE ORDERS OF COLUMNS THAT CHARACTERIZE THE COLOSSEUM.

Date: 72–80 AD

Definition: Known as the Flavian Amphitheater, an elliptical-shaped building that served as an arena for spectacles.

Dimensions: Axes 615 feet and 513.5 feet, inner arena 282 x 177 feet, original height 170 feet.

State of preservation: Long used as a quarry for building materials, subject to more or less voluntary destructive interventions, and now under threat due to structural strain and broadening fissures.

Acknowledgments: UNESCO World Heritage Site since 1980, including the entire historic center of Rome; listed one of the new seven wonders of the world.

LIBRARY OF CELSUS

Location: Ancient Ephesus, Selçuk, district of Izmir, Turkey

TURKEY

The immense façade of the Celsus library, which contained 12,000 volumes and houses the tomb of the Roman senator to whom it is dedicated, recalls a theatrical scene. The double order of columns and the niches for the statues refer, in fact, to a scene from the Ancient Greek theaters, which inspired the building's design. Built by a Roman in a traditionally Greek territory, the library consisted of a single room facing east and enclosed by an apse; below, in a vaulted room the remains of Celsus were laid. The style of the building is heavily influenced by Greek classicism, despite the fact that the materials used are typical of the second century and Roman architectural achievements.

OPPOSITE: THE FAÇADE OF THE LIBRARY OF CELSUS IS INSPIRED BY THEATRICAL SCENERY, CONSISTING OF TWO ORDERS OF PROJECTING COLONNADES THAT CREATE A PLAY OF SHADOWS ON THE WALL BEHIND. IN THE FOUR NICHES OF THE FIRST ORDER STAND THE PERSONIFIED QUALITIES OF CELSUS: WISDOM, BENEVOLENCE, VIRTUE, AND KNOWLEDGE.
BELOW: VIEW FROM THE BOTTOM OF THE PROJECTING COLONNADE.

Date: 110–135 AD

Definition: Library built in honor of Roman senator Tiberius Julius Celsus Polemaeanus.

Dimensions: Building interior measured 55 x 36 feet; it housed 12,000 papyrus scrolls.

State of preservation: The original building was destroyed by two earthquakes; the façade was reconstructed in the 1960s and 1970s by means of anastylosis.

Acknowledgments: Ephesus has been listed a UNESCO World Heritage Site since 1994.

OPPOSITE: OVERVIEW OF THE FAÇADE OF
THE CELSUS LIBRARY AND THE ARCHED
PORTAL LEADING TO THE *AGORÀ*.

HADRIAN'S WALL

Location: Ancient border between Britain and Caledonia (current Scotland)

ENGLAND

For a long time, Hadrian's Wall formed the northernmost border of the Roman Empire and served as the symbol of imperial power in the northern provinces. The wall was part of a larger defensive complex, including a military road along the length of the fortification, two large ditches (armed with rows of pointed stakes), gates serving as customs posts, and a series of fortified signaling towers. The wall was guarded by legionaries, forming a frontier garrison, and auxiliaries. The most famous defensive barrier of the Roman Empire, the *Roman wall* (as it is called today), has become a major visitor attraction of northern England, also very popular with hikers, as it offers an easy, adventurous, as well as historically rich walking route.

OPPOSITE: A SECTION OF ROMAN FORTIFICATION IN THE SCOTTISH TERRITORY, ERECTED IN THE FIRST HALF OF THE SECOND CENTURY AD.
BELOW: DETAIL OF THE STONE ROWS OF HADRIAN'S WALL AND ITS ADJOINING CONSTRUCTIONS. TODAY, IN MANY AREAS, THE WALL NO LONGER EXISTS, BUT IN THE HILLY AND MOUNTAINOUS AREA OF THE CENTRAL ZONE, THE WALL REMAINS INTACT WITH SMALL FORTIFICATIONS AT EVERY MILE (FOR A TOTAL OF APPROXIMATELY EIGHTY SMALLER FORTS AND FOURTEEN LARGER FORTS).

Date: 125 AD–approximately 135 AD

Definition: Fortified wall erected by Roman emperor Hadrian for defense against invasion by the northern tribes.

Dimensions: Length 75 miles, Width 6–10 feet, height 13–16 feet.

State of preservation: With the decline of the Roman Empire, stone from the wall was reused for local construction. Today some ancient sections remain, including the central section, under the safeguard of UNESCO.

Acknowledgments: UNESCO World Heritage Site since 1987.

HAGIA SOPHIA

Location: Istanbul, Turkey

TURKEY

Ancient Constantinople, for a time the capital of the Roman Empire and later of the Byzantine Empire, was a political, religious, and artistic center of extraordinary significance for centuries. At the heart of this magnificent city, Emperor Justinian decided, in 532 AD, to build a grand basilica on the site where two churches had previously been destroyed by an earthquake and a fire, respectively: the result was a marvael of architecture and art. The vast, airy central nave with its complex system of vaults and semi-domes culminate in an enormous grand dome supported by four arches, in the past considered the *dome of paradise*. The interior of the basilica is decorated with polychrome marble, ornamental stone inlay, and gilded finishes. Istanbul has experienced many different cultures: the influences of Byzantium and the Ottoman Empire constitute its two most famous *anime*. The modern city today reflects the features of this dualism, visibly exemplified in the Hagia Sophia, where both realities assemble under a grand dome in perfect synthesis.

OPPOSITE: VIEW OF THE HAGIA SOPHIA, A MASTERPIECE OF BYZANTINE ARCHITECTURE. THE FOUR MINARETS WERE ADDED AT A LATER PERIOD.
BELOW: DECORATION OF THE INTERIOR OF THE MAJESTIC DOME ABOVE THE CENTRAL NAVE, SET ON FOUR LARGE PILLARS. IN THE UPPER SECTION OF THE DOME A SERIES OF WINDOWS AROUND THE CIRCUMFERENCE ILLUMINATE THE INTERIOR, MAKING THE EXQUISITE MOSAIC DECORATION SHINE.

Date: 537 AD (inauguration of the current structure).

Definition: A grand basilica dedicated to Saint Sophia ("Divine Wisdom"), initially consecrated Greek Orthodox, then Catholic, and subsequently becoming a mosque, the building was ultimately converted to a museum.

Dimensions: 246 x 230 feet; the central dome has a diameter of approximately 102 feet and a height of 180 feet from the ground level.

State of preservation: Good.

Acknowledgments: UNESCO World Heritage Site since 1985.

OPPOSITE: MOSAIC OF THE *BASILISSA* IRENE OF ATHENS, EMPRESS OF THE EAST.

CHICHÉN ITZÁ

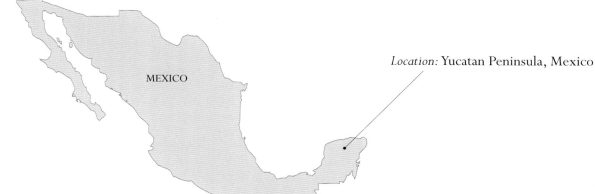

Location: Yucatan Peninsula, Mexico

MEXICO

The great Mayan city of Chichén Itzá emerged at the site of two large natural wells, providing an abundance of water within the arid Yucatan Peninsula and favoring settlement. During the Classic Period of Mayan civilization, the site became a regional capital, ruling the life of the northern plains and neighboring centers and wielding formidable economic power governed by a noble elite. The city holds some extraordinary structures: administrative buildings, places of worship, temples, and a playing field. The most intriguing and well-known structure is the Kukulkan Temple, symbol of Mayan civilization, dedicated to the god Quetzalcoatl: a large pyramid with four imposing stairways, oriented to project the shadow of a feathered snake at sunrise and sunset during the equinoxes.

OPPOSITE: IN THE FOREGROUND, A *CHAC MOOL* STATUE AT THE PRE-COLUMBIAN SITE OF CHICHÉN ITZÁ: THIS TRADITIONAL MESOAMERICAN SCULPTURE DEPICTS A RECLINING FIGURE HOLDING A TRAY ON HIS LAP, PROBABLY DESIGNED FOR SACRIFICIAL OFFERING. BELOW: FRONTAL VIEW OF THE PYRAMID OF KUKULKAN, ALSO CALLED *EL CASTILLO*, DEDICATED TO THE GOD QUETZALCOATL. PP. 72-73: DETAIL OF BAS-RELIEFS THAT ADORN THE ARCHITECTURAL STRUCTURES OF THE CHICHÉN ITZÁ SITE, DEPICTING WARRIORS AND SERPENTS (SYMBOLS OF QUETZALCOATL, THE "FEATHERED SERPENT").

Date: 500 BC–1500 AD

Definition: Great city and regional capital of the Maya.

Dimensions: Approximately one square mile.

State of preservation: Varied. Currently, due to mass tourism, attempts are underway to regulate visitor numbers; since 1972 Mexico has placed all pre-Columbian monuments under its ownership and federal protection.

Acknowledgments: UNESCO World Heritage Site since 1988; listed one of the new seven wonders of the world.

KIYOMIZU-DERA TEMPLE

Location: Kyoto, Japan

JAPAN

The inspired beauty of the Otowa-san Kiyomizu-dera complex is timeless. The large temple, constructed on a hill overlooking Kyoto is surrounded by enchanting nature, pristine waterfalls, and cherry blossom trees: a symbol of an essential and deeply balanced architecture characteristic of Ancient Japan. The halls of the temple, designed to welcome pilgrims, illuminate a warm light in the evening that contrasts with the surrounding nature. Underneath the main hall, dedicated to the goddess of compassion, Kannon, lies the Otowa waterfall, from which the temple acquires its name: according to legend, the waters offer health, longevity, and wisdom.

OPPOSITE: FRONTAL VIEW OF THE WESTERN GATE OF KYOTO'S KIYOMIZU-DERA COMPLEX. BELOW: THE PAVILIONS WITH CHARACTERISTIC PAGODA ROOFS STAND OUT AMONG THE RICH VEGETATION NOURISHED BY THE BENEFICIAL WATERS. PP. 76-77: THE MAIN HALL OF THE KIYOMIZU-DERA TEMPLE HAS A LARGE PORTICO SUPPORTED BY HUNDREDS OF COLUMNS EXTENDING OVER THE SLOPE, OFFERING A BEAUTIFUL PANORAMIC VIEW OF THE CITY.

Date: 798 AD–1633 AD

Definition: Buddhist temple known as Otowa-san Kiyomizu-dera, part of a larger religious complex.

Descriptive Features: The temple terrace is supported by 139 pillars overhanging the mountain slope, constructed without the use of a single nail.

State of preservation: Good; supported by tourism.

Acknowledgments: UNESCO World Heritage Site since 1994; among the finalists for the new seven wonders of the world.

THE MOAI

EASTER ISLAND

CHILE

Location: Easter Island, Chile

The enigmatic statues that populate the coasts of Easter Island have always found themselves at the center of theories and legends for their presence and conformation. Made from up to eighty-ton megalithic blocks of tufa and transported from quarries *to stand* at the coast, these solemn-looking visages, sometimes topped with a *pukao* (a top-knot of long red hair), reveal little of their meaning. The most common theory purports that these colossal statues were built by the Polynesian people between the eleventh and sixteenth century AD, with propitiatory intent: their proximity to the coast would provide the promise of abundant fishing. It is likely, however, that these faces portray prominent figures of the community or ancestors imbued with a sacral aura. Beyond the meaning of the intriguing inscriptions in Rongorongo glyphs, as of yet not deciphered, the Moai standing vigil over the land and sea remain undeniably fascinating for their mystery as well as their beauty.

OPPOSITE: ENIGMATIC PROFILES OF THE MOAI OF RAPA NUI.
BELOW: SOME OF THE TRADITIONAL MONOLITHIC STATUES OF EASTER ISLAND HAVE BEEN, OVER TIME, COMPLETELY OR PARTIALLY BURIED.

Date: XI–XVI century AD

Definizione: Anthropomorphic monolithic statues in basalt tufa aligned along the coast.

Height: Between 8 and 33 feet.

State of preservation: Subject to heavy erosion, however, all but two remain in situ in their original position; one Moai statue is housed in Hamburg and the other at the British Museum in London. For some time, the island has been subject to excessive tourist pressures, which places the island and the statues in a precarious balance between conservation and tourism.

Acknowledgments: Rapa Nui National Park has been listed a UNESCO World Heritage Site since 1995.

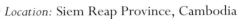

ANGKOR WAT

CAMBODIA

Location: Siem Reap Province, Cambodia

The heart of Cambodia is the temple of Angkor Wat, official symbol and source of national pride, and the emblem of classic Khmer architecture. The temple is a traditional mountain temple, representing Mount Meru (home of the gods): constructed in a rectangular shape, surrounded by a wide moat symbolizing the ocean, while the five central towers recall the five peaks of the sacred mountain. Significantly, the temple is oriented to the west: the West symbolizes the *sunset* of life, leading scholars to agree that the temple was, first and foremost, a place of burial. This idea was confirmed by the counter-clockwise design of the magnificent bas-reliefs of the temple, a practice that finds precedents in ancient Hindu funerary rites. Vishnu is often associated with the West, and it is now commonly accepted that Angkor Wat would have probably served as both a temple and a royal mausoleum. The harmony of the temple is comparable to that of classical architecture, characterized by a balance of proportion emblematic of all the structures of the complex. Characteristic decorative elements include the enchanting *apsaras*, feminine divinities, bas-reliefs depicting scenes from epic poems, narrative and floral scenes on the pediments, and, at one time, golden-stucco and wood-paneled ceilings and doors (now lost). The vegetation surrounding the building, sometimes engulfing the architectural structures, enhances the mysterious fascination of the site.

OPPOSITE: TRADITIONAL OGIVAL TOWERS (IN THE FORM OF A LOTUS BUD) FLANK A STAIRWAY AT ANGKOR WAT.
BELOW: A GLIMPSE OF STATUES AT ANGKOR WAT EXPRESSING A SOLEMN, OTHERWORLDLY GAZE.

Date: 1113–1150 AD

Definition: Khmer Temple, perhaps mausoleum for King Suryavarman II.

Surface area: 155 square miles.

State of preservation: In the fourteenth or the fifteenth century, the temple was converted to a Theravada Buddhist temple. In the twentieth century, it underwent extensive restoration to halt the advancement of vegetation, which tended to engulf the structures; restoration work was interrupted in the 1970s and 1980s because of the civil war and the Khmer Rouge dictatorship.

Acknowledgments: The temple is present on Cambodia's flag; it is one of the largest religious sites in the world and a UNESCO World Heritage Site since 1992.

Pp. 82-83: The temple of Angkor Wat, representation of the house of the gods, develops in levels, horizontally (the walls and surrounding moat symbolize the mountains and ocean, the nucleus of the dwelling) and vertically (access to the higher areas become gradually more exclusive and reserved).
Pp. 84-85: The entrance to the temple of Ta Prohm in Angkor emanates an almost preternatural fascination, in no small part due to the giant roots engulfing the stone and the surrounding jungle.

THE FORBIDDEN CITY

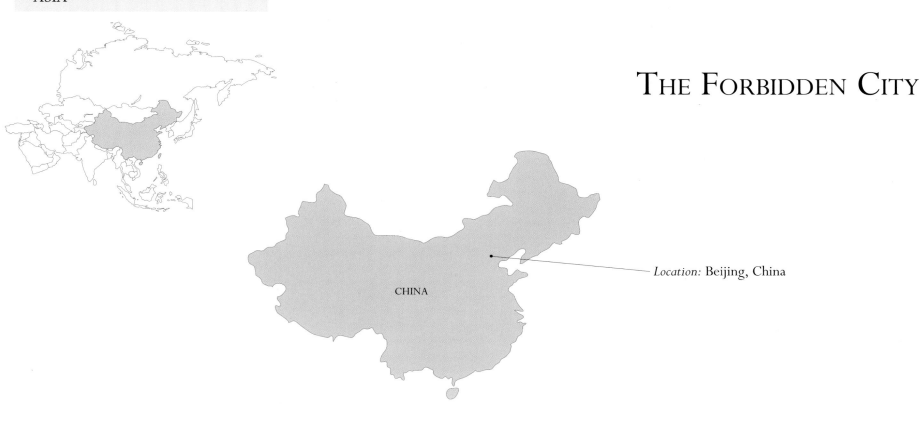

Location: Beijing, China

CHINA

The Forbidden City, located in the heart of Beijing, is considered the "largest building in the world." Every detail of the site is a reminder of the greatness of the most powerful dynasties in China's history: 980 buildings, 26-foot perimeter walls, corner towers with intricate roofs boasting 72 ridges, massive doors decorated with gold nails, opulent palaces adorned in bas-relief, dragons depicted on the vaults of the ceilings, and imperial seals all strictly observe symbolic and religious principles. The Forbidden City represents the height of Chinese classical architecture, profoundly influencing successive architectural developments.

OPPOSITE: A PAVILION OF THE IMPERIAL PALACE OVERLOOKS THE REFLECTING POOL AT SUNRISE.
BELOW: THE MONUMENTAL ENTRANCE TO THE FORBIDDEN CITY, KNOWN AS THE *GUGONG* ("FORMER PALACE"), IS TODAY THE MOST EXTENSIVE AND FINEST PRESERVED RESIDENCE OF THE IMPERIAL FAMILY.

Date: 1406–1420 AD

Definition: Imperial Palace of the Ming and Qing dynasties, referred to today as *Gugong* ("former palace").

Dimensions: The complex covers 178 acres.

State of preservation: Good; since 1925 the complex has been a museum.

Acknowledgments: UNESCO World Heritage Site since 1987.

OPPOSITE: THE FORBIDDEN CITY IN THE
HEART OF BEIJING IS SURROUNDED (AND
ISOLATED) BY TURRETED WALLS AND A MOAT
THAT REFLECTS THE COLORS OF THE ROOFS.
PP. 90-91: DETAIL FROM THE WALL OF THE
NINE DRAGONS, CONSISTING OF BRIGHTLY
GLAZED BRICKS IN SEVEN COLORS AND
REPRESENTING NINE DRAGONS PLAYING AMONG
THE CLOUDS, LOCATED IN THE IMPERIAL
GARDEN OF BEIHAI PARK, IN THE NORTHWEST
SECTION OF THE FORBIDDEN CITY.

PERU

MACHU PICCHU

Location: 70 miles northeast of Cuzco, Urubamba Province, Peru

Architecture is perhaps the greatest expression of Incan art. Isolated in the clouds of the Andes, Machu Picchu is one of the few places in the world where the architecture of the Inca remains relatively intact. This *lost city* acquires its name from the rocky peak called *Machu Picchu*, which in Quechua means "ancient mountain." Machu Picchu remained unknown to the outside world until 1911, when it was discovered by American archaeologist Hiram Bingham. Given the location at such a remarkable elevation, it is probable the city served primarily as a religious center, a sort of sacred residence for the Incan emperor Pachacútec; the population was mobile and varied, belonging to an elite in the residential area and, in the agricultural area, with settlers from lands conquered by the Inca. The Incan civil war of 1531 and the Spanish Conquest brought an end to Machu Picchu's golden age. The settlers who lived in the city, indentured to serve the emperor, took advantage of the city's moment of weakness to return to their lands of origin, and the highest social class followed the king into exile. The city develops on a series of terraces along several levels: in the south the agricultural area and in the north the urban center, rich in vestiges once belonging to buildings of worship and ritual and to residences, including a *sacred square* constructed in accordance with astronomical alignments. In 2009, the complex recorded a record 2 million visitors.

OPPOSITE: AERIAL VIEW OF A SECTION OF THE MACHU PICCHU SITE, REVEALING THE REMARKABLE LAYOUT OF THE BUILDINGS, LOCATED ON SEVERAL TERRACES TO MAKE THE MOST OF THE PLATEAU SLOPES.
BELOW: THE WALLS OF THE MACHU PICCHU CONSTRUCTIONS ARE BUILT DRY, WITHOUT THE USE OF MORTAR. THE IRREGULAR STONES CONFER A REMARKABLE STABILITY TO THE BUILDINGS, ABLE TO WITHSTAND THE FREQUENT EARTHQUAKES THAT MAKE THE EARTH TREMBLE IN THE ANDEAN MOUNTAINS.

Date: 1438 –1471 (foundation), inhabited until 1532.

Definition: Ancient city of the Inca founded on the rocky cliff uniting the mountains of Machu Picchu and Huayna Picchu.

Surface area: 5 square miles; elevation, approximately 7,972 feet.

State of preservation: Discovered at the beginning of the twentieth century, the original structures were missing roofs and engulfed by vegetation. The excavations of 1912 –1915 brought to light archaeological remains, illegally exported, which have yet to be returned to the Peruvian authorities. Tourism, since the 1950s, has been extensive: beyond the positive visibility, the influx has jeopardized the condition of the site. Since 2005, a general plan for sustainable development has been adopted and visitor numbers regulated.

Acknowledgments: UNESCO World Heritage Site since 1983. In 2007 Machu Picchu was listed one of the new seven wonders of the world.

OPPOSITE: THE CITADEL OF MACHU
PICCHU WAS BUILT ON THE BACK OF A
PROTRUDING SPUR IN THE MIDDLE SECTION
OF A MOUNTAIN IN THE CORDILLERA
DE VILCABAMBA. PERUVIAN SCHOLAR
ALFONSINA BARRIONUEVO REMARKS, THE
SITE "SUSPENDS ITS BUILDINGS AND TEMPLES
ON THE GRANITE CANYON OF URUBAMBA,
HANGING ABOVE THE RIVER."

WONDERS OF THE MODERN WORLD

When the New Open World Corporation launched a global referendum in 2000 to nominate the *New Seven Wonders of the World*, the initial number of seventeen candidates soon bourgeoned into 150, and the closing of the referendum, under formidable pressure from public opinion throughout the world, came to be postponed more than once. Exactly seven years later, on the symbolic date of July 7, 2007, the final list of seven architectural works was made public, attesting to the modern world's ardent interest in the subject and the exceptional difficulty of selecting so few indisputable symbols from, what is now, a *mare magnum* of extraordinary cultural testimonies of human history and ingenuity. The *new seven wonders*, however, are not *new* at all. The far-reaching objective and overall requirement for the compendium was to offer an alternative to the original list, including visible, time-honored works and all geographical, chronological, and cultural perspectives. A natural consequence of this criteria is that the *new* wonders of the world have been drawn from remote as well as contemporary history, crossing but not coinciding with the *wonders* of the modern world.

Reference to the *modern world* seems ever more a general designation. The historiographical concept of *modernity* and, subsequently, of *contemporaneity*, refers to the many centuries from the end of the Middle Ages to today. Considering the planet as a whole, the boundaries of historiography come to be viewed from a more malleable perspective, since there is no self-contained, discrete evolution in the history of culture and civilizations in any part of the world. Rather than rigorously considering a chronological demarcation, for the first phase of modern history (XI–XVI century AD) consideration will be dedicated to the difference between the vestiges of the past that have a continuity of use (designating them to the present in their original urban and cultural location) and the vestiges that form part of the purely archaeological sphere. By this principle of designation, the Piazza dei Miracoli of Pisa, with its original layout from 1063 and long life of modifications and renovations, functioning continuously into the twenty-first century, would be designated a modern wonder, as opposed to Machu Picchu, constructed in the fifteenth century but falling distinctly within the category of archaeological structures, far removed from new development, engulfed in vegetation, and *forgotten* for nearly 400 years.

The functional variation in the wonders of the modern world informs another aspect that renders designation a complex, as well as fascinating, undertaking. The functional differences already observed for ancient wonders are amplified in modern monuments given the great expansion of geographic and cultural horizons. From the earliest evidence of still rather remote times (XI–XVII centuries), in which buildings of worship and mausoleums predominated, as we approach the present the more the categories intertwine, including government buildings, private residences, monuments symbolic of the new urban metropolises, infrastructures testifying to industrial innovation, and functional buildings: the new captivations of a globalized society. After all, the last two hundred years of history have been marked by rapid change. The Industrial Revolution, the abolition of slavery, the immigration boom, the movements and achievements of the people, and two world wars have altered the course of human history and, accordingly, architectural thought. The wonders of the modern world testify to these changes and, at the same time, recall the darkest chapters of modern history with sites commemorating the struggles for freedom, justice, and human rights.

On an ideal journey through this wondrous reality, it would serve the traveler well to follow thematic and chronological criteria, while ignoring the rigidity of the subdivision. In this sense, it is natural to be attracted to the incredible achievements of Italian architecture, pioneer of the Old World in the history of art. The Tower of Pisa, completed in 1350, icon of Italian architecture and unique symbol in the world, involving its peculiar form, arouses a curiosity that cultivates, over time, the tower's iconic and universal fame. With the extraordinary beauty of the buildings that surround it, Pisa's entire Piazza

OPPOSITE: THE TOP FLOOR OF THE ICONIC STATUE OF LIBERTY, A TRUE SYMBOL OF MODERN WONDERS.
PP. 98-99: THE SYDNEY OPERA HOUSE WITH ITS DISTINCTIVE WHITE SAILS RISES AT ONE END OF SYDNEY HARBOUR BRIDGE, A THROUGH ARCH BRIDGE ACROSS THE BAY, OVERLOOKING THE CITY.
PP. 100-101: FROM THE VERTIGINOUS HEIGHTS OF THE TALLEST BUILDING IN THE WORLD, THE BURJ KHALIFA OFFERS A SPECTACULAR PANORAMA OF DUBAI'S FUTURISTIC BUILDINGS.

dei Miracoli has been designated a UNESCO World Heritage Site since 1987. The piazza seems a verdant island from which emerge with unexpected candor some of the most beautiful jewels of Italian architecture. The rich decoration of the Duomo, in the Romanesque style with polychrome marble, mosaics, pointed arches, massive bronze doors, and a magnificent dome, express in every detail the will to create pure, harmonious masterpieces, in the search of lines most consonant with the evocation of Pisa's greatness as a maritime power of the Mediterranean. Here is how a building of worship becomes, at the same time, a celebration of its patrons, be they individuals, empires, kingdoms, or cities.

For the celebration of power, Venice offers another of the great wonders of Italy: Basilica San Marco. Before consecrated a cathedral in 1807, the building served for centuries as a palatine church for the nearby ducal palace, magnificent seat of the doge in the Venetian Gothic style. Beyond the many vicissitudes the building has undergone in its long history, it is enough to turn the corner of Piazza San Marco to witness the wonder of it. The polychrome façade reveals mosaics, bas-reliefs, and chiaroscuro in an opulent play of volumes, arches, and vaults, doors in bronze, decorated lunettes, and the *triumphal quadriga* of horses at the main portal. The wonder exists, beyond the artistic and cultural value of the work, in profound emotional reaction: the inevitable sense of wonder before the intricacy of detail and harmony of form, a large jewel set between the piazza (small and elegant like a Venetian lounge) and the lagoon just beyond.

Far from Italy but sharing with the basilica a masterful construction of a dome is the wonder found in India:

the Taj Mahal, a masterpiece of Islamic art. An enduring memory of eternal love, built by the emperor Shah Jahan for his wife, the Taj Majal fits form with function according to one of the original categories of the seven wonders of the ancient world: it is a mausoleum, like the Mausoleum at Halicarnassus from which the architectural genre derives its name. The beauty of the Taj Mahal is highly scenic. The reiteration of the square form, a symbol of perfection in Islamic art, merges with the soft and curved lines of the ogival arches and dome. The impressive view of the mausoleum from the front is amplified by the building's reflection in the water reservoir before it, and the sense of isolation of the structure, at the center of a large garden, reinforces its imposing grandeur.

The privilege of a globalized world allows us on this ideal journey to travel in a blink of an eye from the majesty of the Taj Mahal in India to the grand opulence of the court of the Sun King in France. Only a few decades after the Taj Mahal was built, the Palace of Versailles took form and shape, one of the most extraordinary palaces in Europe and the world. The residence of the sovereign of France offers an unforgettable wonder: 2,000 acres of land adorned with elaborate English gardens (water displays, fountains, statues, flora, and ornamentation), magnificent palaces and pavilions, breathtaking gilded and mirrored halls, and masterpieces of art in profusion establish Versailles as a symbol of wealth, power, and the most refined sophistication. A few years later, it became possible to see a Russian version of Versailles: Peterhof Palace, the royal residence commissioned by Peter the Great, engages the same opulent forms and ostentatious splendor, rendering evanescent the border between

private residence and center of power and arousing a sense of unprecedented awe and wonder. Different lines characterize another impressive royal residence: Neuschwanstein Castle, built at the end of the nineteenth century in Bavaria by and for King Ludwig II, amazes for its fairytale, magical, and unique atmosphere. Located on a mountain, at the edge of vertiginous precipice surrounded by forest, the castle's towers rise, up to 263 feet, against the sky, the arduous and talented work of the architect and two scenographers.

Since the mid-nineteenth century, there has been a trend reversal in architectural realizations. Following the era of great religious buildings and constructions of secular power, the industrial revolution and social upheaval shifted attention toward new symbols, with the result of a world poised at the gates of contemporary history. There are no better icons emblematic of this era than the Statue of Liberty and the Eiffel Tower, constructed a few years apart, driving forth the Old and New World respectively, resonating a reality in flux. The imposing statue overlooking Manhattan Bay, visible as far as twenty-five miles away, is the symbol of a society in transformation: freedom gained with independence and dramatic, hopeful, stories of immigrants arriving at the port of Ellis Island converge in a single place, epitomizing the achievements and contradictions of modern society. The fame of the Eiffel Tower, on the other side of the Atlantic, immortalizes the memory of the Paris Exposition of 1889 (centenary of the French Revolution) and the great achievements of industrialization and scientific progress, the new reality of machines that led the way to define the twentieth century. The great wonder of these monuments is manifest in their forms,

impressive in and of themselves, resonating their history, the values that conceived them, the echo of their past that bears fruit in the culture of the present.

On this ideal journey, we enter the twentieth century with another great symbolic monument: Christ the Redeemer in Rio de Janeiro, which, like the Statue in New York, stands vigil over a city in a globalized, multicultural, and colorful world, replete with contradictions and wondrous diversity. Through the twentieth century, it is impossible, aside the symbolic, to ignore functionality, the necessity to respond to the increasingly pressing demands of the contemporary world. The oppressive traffic of San Francisco motivates the construction of the magnificent Golden Gate Bridge, with its characteristic orange color emerging from the fog, born of practical need to become, only later, a symbol of the city. Necessity also motivated the city of Sydney to create a space dedicated to art and musical performance, the splendid Opera House, its sails set white against the blue of the harbor.

The twenty-first century is experiencing the proliferation of avant-garde symbols. Dubai's Burj Khalifa skyscraper, 2,722 feet high, combines functionality with pure ostentation, an extravagant, record-breaking work of modernity. The wonder of this extraordinary work of engineering is emblematic of a contemporary society that seeks the future: ambitious, free, and driven.

PIAZZA DEI MIRACOLI

ITALY

Location: Pisa, Italy

The Piazza dei Miracoli in Pisa holds unique fascination: few places in the world can epitomize so richly and comprehensively within its space the beauty of Italian art and the echo of Italy's long and glorious history. The area northwest of the city walls is a vast green space where, one after the other, splendid monuments emerge that symbolize the fundamental stages of human life: the baptistery represents birth; the Duomo, in the quintessential expression of the Pisane-Romanesque style, life; and the Camposanto, death. Beyond rises the legendary tower of Pisa, for many foreigners the symbol of the whole of Italy, erected as a bell tower, its higher stories today closed to the public because of its characteristic slope, which adds a curious attraction to its artistic and architectural aesthetic. The style of the cathedral reflects many different influences: Romanesque, Byzantine, and Islamic elements testify to the great maritime republic Pisa was at the time.

OPPOSITE: IN PIAZZA DEI MIRACOLI, DETAIL OF THE LEANING TOWER OF PISA, BELL TOWER OF THE CATHEDRAL DEDICATED TO SAINT MARY OF THE ASSUMPTION.
BELOW: OVERVIEW OF THE WHITE MONUMENTS OF PIAZZA DEI MIRACOLI, WONDER OF ITALIAN ART.
P. 104: DECORATIVE CAPITAL OF THE CATHEDRAL WITH SPLENDID MARBLE INLAY.
P. 105: REGAL GOTHIC TABERNACLE OVER THE ENTRANCE OF PISA'S CAMPOSANTO ("HOLY FIELD"), DEPICTING THE *VIRGIN AND CHILD AND FOUR SAINTS*, WORK OF A FOLLOWER OF GIOVANNI PISANO (XIV CENTURY).

Date: Initial construction, 1063; most recent modifications, early XX century.

Definition: Piazza of the Duomo in the historic center of Pisa.

Dimensions: Cathedral, 315 feet (central nave) x 236 feet (transept), height 168.3 feet with the dome; baptistery, circumference 351.84 feet, base width 8.63 feet, height 179.99 feet; tower, height 183.77 feet.

Descriptive features: The baptistery is the largest in Italy; the tower leans approximately 16.5 feet from vertical at its highest point. According to legend, Galileo Galilei expressed his theories on the motion of the pendulum by observing the chandelier of the Duomo. The name *Piazza dei Miracoli* was attributed to the complex by Gabriele d'Annunzio in 1910 and is often mistaken with *Campo dei Miracoli*, a fairytale location belonging to the story of *Pinocchio*.

Acknowledgments: UNESCO World Heritage Site since 1987.

THE TAJ MAHAL

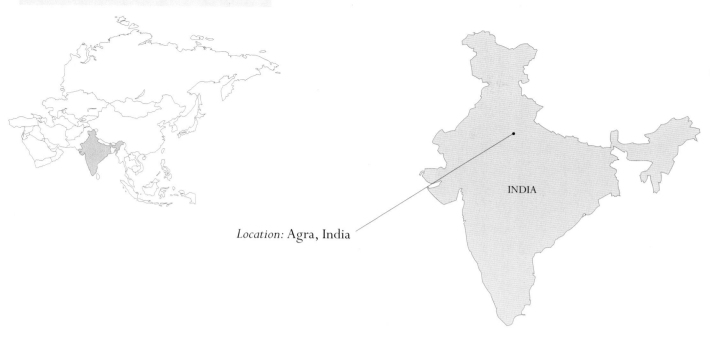

INDIA

Location: Agra, India

The view of the famous Taj Mahal reflected in the water is one of the most iconic of Islamic Mughal art and one of the most famous wonders of the world. The splendid mausoleum, symbol of the emperor's eternal love for his bride, reveals its unmistakable symmetrical physiognomy within a large rectangular enclosure at the end of a vast garden, called the *Garden of Paradise*, against which the white of the marble dominates the surrounding landscape. Adjoining the west bank of the Yamuna River (diverted to achieve a more impressive scenic effect), the main building emerges on a raised foundation bordered at the corners by minarets and surmounted by a traditional onion dome. Each feature contributes to create an impression of abundant wealth and a grand visual impact. The interior of the mausoleum is adorned with intricate marble inlay and delicate bas-relief, embellished by decoration made of materials that evoke distant countries: jade and crystal from China, carnelian from Arabia, and lapis lazuli from Afghanistan.

OPPOSITE: : THE DECORATION OF THE TAJ MAHAL IS THE EXTRAORDINARY ACHIEVEMENT OF THE BUILDING'S MUGHAL ARCHITECTURE. THE MARBLE THAT CHARACTERIZES THE ISLAMIC ARCHED WINDOWS PRESENTS A FINELY CARVED AND INLAID FLORAL DECORATION OF INCREDIBLE DETAIL.
BELOW: THE FRONTAL VIEW OF THE TAJ MAHAL REVEALS THE BEAUTY INHERENT IN ITS PERFECT SYMMETRY.
PP. 108-109: DETAIL OF THE TAJ MAHAL, SHOWING THE CENTRAL DOME, ONE OF THE FOUR MINOR DOMES, AND ONE OF THE FOUR MINARETS.

Date: 1631–1648

Definition: Mausoleum built by Mughal emperor Shah Jahan in memory of his favorite wife, Arjumand Banu Begum.

Dimensions: Entire complex approximately 1,900 x 985 feet, height 240 feet.

Descriptive features: The building is located in a square-shaped garden, the geometric form a symbol of perfection in Islamic art. The course of the Yamuna River was diverted to reflect the outline of the mausoleum in the morning. It is said that over 1,000 elephants and buffaloes were used during construction for the transport of raw materials.

Acknowledgments: UNESCO World Heritage Site since 1983.

ITALY

BASILICA SAN MARCO

Location: Venice, Italy

Basilica San Marco is not only the most important church in Venice but also the city's cathedral since 1807 and the seat of the Patriarch. The wondrous basilica, overlooking Piazza San Marco and adjacent to the ducal palace, dates to the eleventh century. Construction began under the doge Domenico Contarini in 1063, and the basilica was consecrated in 1094. Construction, however, was not completed until 1617, when the two altars were installed. Because of the protracted length of construction and numerous renovations over the centuries, the art and architecture of the basilica cannot be assigned a single definitive style, rather becoming a sort of Romanesque-Byzantine and Gothic hybrid with evident Eastern influences: in short, a self-contained work extraordinary in its unique eclecticism. The marvelous façade in marble, realized in the thirteenth century, includes five portals and a terraced upper story. The central portal is the most elaborately decorated, surmounted by the famous *triumphal quadriga*, four horses in bronze plundered from Constantinople by the Venetians at the end of the Fourth Crusade. While the prevalent color of the exterior is white despite the polychromatic decoration of the lunettes, the interior shines almost entirely golden in a complexity of spectacular mosaics and housing works of inestimable value, such as the Pala D'oro on the main altar and the *Tesoro di San Marco* (Treasure of Saint Mark), nearly three hundred pieces in gold, silver, glass, and other precious materials. The opulence of the basilica is unforgettable and the view from Piazza San Marco equally so.

OPPOSITE: IN VENICE, THE EXTRAORDINARY FAÇADE OF THE BASILICA SAN MARCO OVERLOOKING PIAZZA SAN MARCO. THE FAÇADE IS DIVIDED INTO TWO ORDERS WITH A TERRACE AND THE LEGENDARY *TRIUMPHAL QUADRIGA* IN BRONZE, TRANSPORTED FROM CONSTANTINOPLE.
BELOW: ONE OF THE EXTERIOR ARCHES OF THE BASILICA SAN MARCO DECORATED IN BAS-RELIEF.
PP. 112-113: AERIAL VIEW OF THE FIVE DOMES OF THE VENETIAN BASILICA, IN THE FORM OF THE GREEK CROSS, TESTIFYING TO ITS EASTERN INFLUENCES.
PP. 114-115: SUPERBLY DECORATED ARCHES ON THE SOUTHERN SIDE OF THE BASILICA.

Date: 1617, completion of the present building.

Definition: Originally conceived as a palatine church annexed to the ducal palace, Basilica San Marco is a cathedral dedicated to Saint Mark (1807) and the principal church of Venice.

Dimensions: 251 x 205 feet (at the transept); height to the dome, 141 feet (92.36 feet in the interior).

Descriptive features: One of the most famous symbols of Venice and the whole of Italy, the building's design privileged the width to more effectively distribute the weight on the sandy ground on which it rises. The polychromy is due to the large amount of raw material used; the layout, a Greek cross, is surmounted by five large Byzantine-style domes, located at the center and at the axes of the cross; the porphyry rhombus on the floor of the atrium in front of the main portal marks the exact spot where Frederick I, Holy Roman Emperor, knelt before Pope Alexander III in 1177.

Acknowledgments: Venice and its lagoon have been listed a UNESCO World Heritage Site since 1987.

PALACE OF VERSAILLES

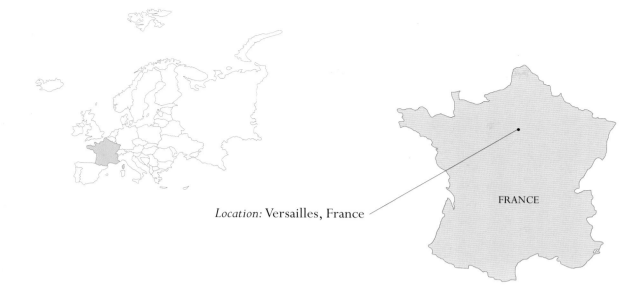

Location: Versailles, France

FRANCE

When in the mid-seventeenth century Louis XIV identified his Versailles hunting estate as the perfect residence for the court far from the confusion of the center of Paris, he was already planning to construct one of the most lavish and incredible buildings ever built. Located on the outskirts of the village of Versailles, approximately twelve miles southwest of the French capital, the baroque castle became the true political seat of the kingdom and residence of the royal court from 1682 to 1789, the year when revolutionaries massacred the royal guard and dragged Louis XVI and Marie Antoinette to their tragic fate. Subsequently, the residence was transformed into a museum dedicated to the history of France by order of Louis Phillippe, and in the current day, the French president will sometimes receive official guests there. The Palace of Versailles is a remarkable masterpiece of French art and architecture of the seventeenth century, consisting of an enchanting succession of halls and corridors lavishly decorated in gold, marble, mirror, and crystal, reflecting the greatness of the Sun King and his spirit of ostentation. The building and its *dépendence* extend for over 2,000 acres, with English gardens embellished with water features, statues, artificial ponds, and incredible fountains of classical inspiration, works by architect André Le Nôtre. Every detail of Versailles evokes an age of splendor and wonder.

OPPOSITE: THE GARDENS OF VERSAILLES, EXTENSIVE AND LAVISH, FOLLOW THE CLASSICAL STYLE, ARTICULATED IN GEOMETRIC SHAPES: FLOWERBEDS, PATHS, AVENUES, HEDGES, SCULPTURES, AND FOUNTAINS AND WATER DISPLAYS OF EXTRAORDINARY BEAUTY.
BELOW: A SUMPTUOUS HALL AT THE PALACE OF VERSAILLES, DISPLAYING A PORTRAIT OF MARIE ANTOINETTE AND HER CHILDREN, WORK OF ÉLISABETH VIGÉE-LE BRUN (1787), THE QUEEN'S OFFICIAL PAINTER.

Date: Initial construction 1661, with extension work by order of Louis XIV.

Definition: Palace constructed by Louis XIV of France (the Sun King), ambitious to demonstrate his power to the world.

Size: The palace covers an area of 721,206 square feet; 1,976 acres is dedicated to the gardens.

Descriptive features: The palace comprises several buildings and gardens, including the central palace, the Grand Trianon, and the Petit Trianon; construction lasted fifty years and employed 30,000 workers; the palace contains 700 rooms. The first royal festivities commenced in 1665, and Versailles became the royal residence of the Sun King and his court from 1682 until the French Revolution. On this site, June 28, 1919, the Treaty of Versailles was signed, formally ending the First World War.

Acknowledgments: UNESCO World Heritage Site since 1979.

WONDERS OF THE MODERN WORLD

OPPOSITE: THE HALL OF MIRRORS,
CONSISTING OF NEARLY TWO HUNDRED
MIRRORS, FORMED PART OF THE GREAT
APARTMENTS. THIS *GRAND GALLERY*, AS IT
WAS CALLED IN THE SEVENTEENTH CENTURY,
DAILY FUNCTIONED AS A PLACE OF PASSAGE,
PRESENTATION, AND MEETING, AND WAS
FREQUENTED BY COURTIERS AND GUESTS.
PP. 120-121: GOLD AND MARBLE INLAY
ADORN THE MARVELOUS HALL OF WAR
AT THE PALACE OF VERSAILLES. ON THE
DOMED CEILING THE PERSONIFICATION OF
VICTORIOUS FRANCE DRESSED IN GARMENTS
OF WAR IS DEPICTED; IN THE CENTRAL LOW
RELIEF, LOUIS XIV RIDES HORSEBACK OVER
PRISONERS AT HIS FEET.

119

NEUSCHWANSTEIN CASTLE

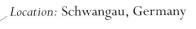

GERMANY

Location: Schwangau, Germany

"The place is one of the most beautiful that can be found, sacred and inaccessible, a temple worthy of You, divine friend, that you would make flourish the salvation and true benediction of the world." So Ludwig II wrote to Richard Wagner in 1868, hoping the composer would soon visit the castle that the king was building in the Bavarian hills as a private *buen retiro* and homage to the great musician. Constructed on the ruins of two previous castles, the manor is perched in a highly scenic position on the edge of a vertiginous gorge, the design of architect Eduard Riedel and scenographers Christian Janck and G. Dollmann, based on the style of the old German feudal castles. A symbol of Bavaria and Germany, legendary for its fairytale aura, the castle contains numerous rooms decorated with Wagnerian motifs and a Byzantine-style throne room, steps in Carrara marble leading to an apse atop which a throne, in gold and ivory, would have been set (a work never realized). A popular visitors' destination for its beauty and surrounding landscape, the royal residence has been one of the most voted-for *wonders* of the modern world.

OPPOSITE, BELOW, AND PP. 124-125: DIFFERENT PERSPECTIVES OF THE FAIRYTALE CASTLE OF NEUSCHWANSTEIN. THE PREDOMINANTLY VERTICAL DEVELOPMENT OF THE SLENDER STRUCTURE OF THE BUILDING AMPLIFIES THE VERTIGINOUS EFFECT OF THE HEIGHTS FROM WHICH IT RISES.

Date: 1869–1886

Definition: Neo-Gothic private residence of King Ludwig II, built on the summit of a steep precipice.

Dimensions: 65,000 square feet, height 213 feet (some towers reach 262 feet).

Descriptive features: One of the most visited castles in Europe and source of inspiration for the fairytale castles of the Disney animated films.

Acknowledgments: Candidate for the seven wonders of the modern world.

STATUE OF LIBERTY

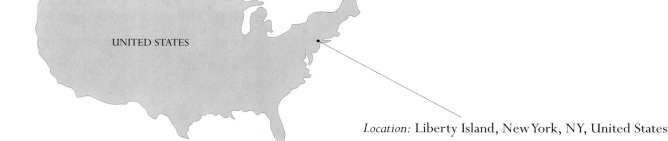

UNITED STATES

Location: Liberty Island, New York, NY, United States

The monumental statue overlooking Manhattan Bay, designed by French sculptor Frédéric Auguste Bartholdi, is the symbol of New York and the United States. Known all over the world, the statue depicts the Roman goddess of liberty wearing a long robe and bearing a torch in her right hand and a book in her left (inscribed with the date of American Independence), and atop her head rests a seven-pointed crown, symbol of the seven seas and the seven continents. At her feet lie broken chains, representing the liberation from slavery. The structure consists of an inner steel framework (work of Gustave Eiffel)—modifying the original design of Viollet-le-Duc (who had intended a brick structure)—and a copper outer casing, reaching a total weight of 225 tons. The statue is hollow and accessible: a climb of 168 steps leads to the crown. Since 1972, the Immigration Museum has been housed in the basement: through the portal of Ellis Island in New York Harbor, immigrants arrived in the late-nineteenth and the early-twentieth century to enter the United States.

OPPOSITE: THE MASSIVE PEDESTAL OF THE STATUE OF LIBERTY, COMPOSED OF A DORIC PLINTH SURMOUNTED BY A NEOCLASSICAL LOGGIA IN REINFORCED CONCRETE AND GRANITE, SUPPORTS THE 225 TONS OF THIS ICONIC TOWERING FIGURE.
BELOW: DETAIL OF THE STATUE OF LIBERTY'S FACE.

Date: 1875

Definition: Monumental statue known as *The Liberty that illuminates the world*, erected to commemorate American Independence (obtained July 4, 1776).

Height: 305 feet.

Descriptive features: One of the most famous monuments in the world and symbol of the United States, the statue was a gift by the French people to the American people, transported in pieces by small ship. The original statue is located in Paris, on the Seine; other copies are found in Tokyo, Las Vegas, and other parts of the world.

Acknowledgments: UNESCO World Heritage Site since 1984.

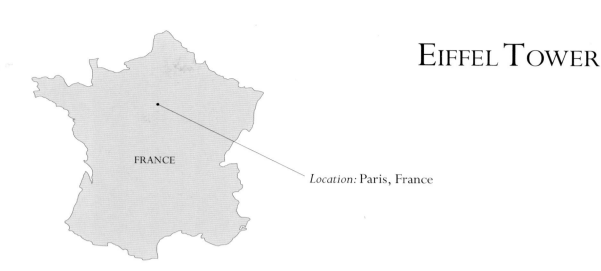

FRANCE

Location: Paris, France

EIFFEL TOWER

Conceived as a temporary structure for the Paris Exposition (World's Fair) of 1889, the Eiffel Tower has for more than 120 years been the symbol of the French capital and one of the most famous icons in the world. The monument carries the name of engineer Alexandre Gustave Eiffel, a civil engineer and architect specializing in metal construction (in particular iron bridges for the railway network), famous for constructing the steel interior framework of the New York Statue of Liberty. In an act of French architectural creativity, Eiffel commissioned two engineers in his company to design a tower inspired by bridge designs: to create a new, modern, purely aesthetic structure in iron. Notwithstanding its great fame today, the Eiffel Tower's story is one of endurance and commitment: contemporaries, both artists and intellectuals, had initially rejected the design as an "ugly skeleton" and "empty candle holder," symbol of a less romantic post-industrial Paris, and petitioned for the tower not to be built. After the Exposition, the structure was to be dismantled, but this purely aesthetic structure had gained functionality, serving as a giant radio antenna, resulting in a stay of execution and establishing it as an integral part of the iconic Parisian landscape.

OPPOSITE AND BELOW: THE LATTICED METAL SKELETON OF THE EIFFEL TOWER IS A TRUE SYMBOL OF PARIS, THE MOST VISITED MONUMENT IN THE WORLD.
PP. 130-131: ON THE SIDE OF THE EIFFEL TOWER OVERLOOKING THE TROCADÉRO, EIGHTEEN OF THE SEVENTY-TWO NAMES ARE ENGRAVED OF THE MOST ILLUSTRIOUS CITIZENS OF PARIS, INCLUDING GEORGES CUVIER, ANTOINE LAVOISIER, AND ANDRÉ-MARIE AMPÈRE.

Date: 1889

Definition: Architectural structure in iron constructed to commemorate the centenary of the French Revolution, built on the occasion of the Paris Exposition of 1889.

Dimensions: Height 1,069 feet (with spire), base width 328 feet.

Descriptive features: To obtain the iron necessary for the construction of its three stories, two and a half million rivets were forged. The tower was the tallest structure in the world for forty years. The third story can be reached by elevator, while the second floor can be reached on foot, over 1,665 steps. The antenna at the summit transmitted in 1908 the first long-distance radio message and today broadcasts thirty radio programs and television channels. Under the balcony, the names of seventy-two French engineers, scientists, and mathematicians are engraved in recognition of these citizens. There are several replicas of the Eiffel Tower in the world, all on a smaller scale with the exception of the Tokyo Tower, a radio tower exceeding the height of the Eiffel Tower by thirty feet.

Acknowledgments: UNESCO World Heritage Site since 1991.

CHRIST THE REDEEMER

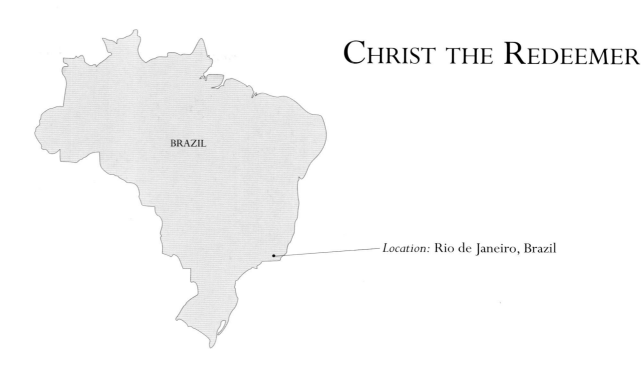

BRAZIL

Location: Rio de Janeiro, Brazil

Few images better represent the whole of Brazil than Christ the Redeemer, overlooking Rio de Janeiro with his open arms and solemn regard, embracing the city that lies at his feet. Built in the twentieth century and inaugurated in 1931, the statue is still considered the largest statue of Christ in the world. Located on Corcovado Mountain in Tijuca National Park, more than 2,300 feet above sea level, Christ the Redeemer offers to any who climb to its base a stunning panorama of the surrounding landscape, consisting of the city Rio de Janeiro and its bay, the unmistakable profile of Sugarloaf Mountain, and the famous beaches of Copacabana and Ipanema. Beneath the benevolent gaze of the enormous Christ, the beauty of the crowded *house of carijó* unfolds.

OPPOSITE: THE TOWERING STATUE OF CHRIST THE REDEEMER OVERLOOKS RIO DE JANEIRO FROM ATOP THE CORCOVADO. BELOW: CLEAN-CUT AND PRECISE LINES CHARACTERIZE THE FAMOUS MONUMENT, DESIGNED BY SCULPTOR PAUL LANDOWSKI.

Date: 1931 (inauguration).

Definition: Statue in soapstone and concrete of Jesus Christ.

Height: 125 feet (including pedestal).

Descriptive features: To realize this monument, the French sculptor Paul Landowski involved several artists in the work, including Leonida Gheorghe, who was assigned the task of sculpting Christ's face; work convened in 1921 during the celebration of Brazil's centenary of independence and cost the equivalent of 3 million US dollars; the weight of the monument exceeds one thousand tons.

Acknowledgments: The statue was listed one of the new seven wonders of the world in 2007 and the whole city of Rio de Janeiro a UNESCO World Heritage Site in 2012.

GOLDEN GATE BRIDGE

UNITED STATES

Location: San Francisco, United States

The great bridge across the Golden Gate, the mile-wide strait between San Francisco Bay and the Pacific Ocean, is one of California's most famous icons and also one of the busiest places of the city, with three lanes running in each direction, along one of the longest highways in the country, the legendary US Route 101. Prior to the bridge's construction, reaching Marin County from San Francisco required a ferry to transport passengers across the strait, but to respond to the ever-mounting traffic, engineer Joseph Baermann Strauss began designing a large suspension bridge in 1927. Ten years later, on May 28, 1937, at noon precisely, President Franklin D. Roosevelt from his office in Washington declared the bride open to the world. The Golden Gate Bridge, a suspension bridge, is constructed by design so that the deck is suspended by long steel ropes from the main cables which are supported by the towers. Until 1964 the Golden Gate Bridge was the longest suspension bridge in the world, and, with its characteristic color of *international orange*, it remains an iconic symbol of the city of San Francisco and the state of California.

OPPOSITE AND BELOW: THE DISTINCTIVE ORANGE COLOR OF THE ACRYLIC COATING ON THE GOLDEN GATE BRIDGE MAKES THE BRIDGE PERFECTLY VISIBLE, EVEN IN FOG OR AT NIGHT.

Date: 1937 (inauguration).

Definition: Suspension bridge connecting San Francisco with Marin County.

Dimensions: Length 8,980 feet, width 90 feet; tower height, 750 feet.

Descriptive features: At the time of construction, the Golden Gate Bridge had the tallest suspension towers in the world. The color of the bridge is called *international orange*, chosen because it makes the structure more visible in the fog. This construction has come to be recognized as a place where suicides occur (possible due to the low protection barriers).

Acknowledgments: The bridge has been designated one of the modern wonders of the world by the Association of American Civil Engineers.

SYDNEY OPERA HOUSE

AUSTRALIA

Location: Sydney, Australia

The Sydney Opera House, overlooking Sydney Harbour, is considered the Australian icon par excellence. Designed by Danish architect Jørn Utzon, with its characteristic overlapping roof in the form of spherical shells (recalling the sails of boats that often pass through the port) and ultra-modern lines, the opera house has just turned forty-five. The main hall of the complex, which rises beside Harbour Bridge, is the Concert Hall, with interiors in wood and assimilating the heights of a cathedral. The theater is the second largest hall and can host an audience of approximately 1,500. The construction of this Australian symbol was both significant and costly: the initial budget of 7 million Australian dollars grew until finally reaching 102 million. The work has established the Sydney Opera House as the icon of the city and of Australia, famous throughout the world, an example of architecture that has left its mark on the twentieth century. The Opera House has been listed a UNESCO World Heritage Site since 2007.

OPPOSITE: THE SPHERICAL SHELLS OF THE SYDNEY OPERA HOUSE RECALL A FLEET OF SAILBOATS ANCHORED IN THE DEEP BLUE OF THE HARBOR.
BELOW: THE CHARACTERISTIC *SAILS* ARE COMPOSED OF CONCRETE RIBS COVERED IN WHITE TILE AND ENCLOSED IN THE FRONT BY TALL WINDOWS THAT FLOOD THE INTERIOR WITH LIGHT. BY ESTIMATE, ABOUT 2,400 PREFABRICATED *RIBS* WERE USED, BUILT ON A CONSTRUCTION SITE AND THEN MOUNTED ON THE BUILDING.
PP. 138-139: THE SYDNEY OPERA HOUSE, SYMBOL OF THE WHOLE OF AUSTRALIA, STANDS ON THE ARTIFICIAL PROMONTORY OF BENNELONG POINT, IN A SCENIC LOCATION.

Date: 1973 (inauguration).

Definition: A spectacular building (recalling white sails) overlooking Sydney Harbour.

Dimensions: The concert hall holds 2,700 seats.

Descriptive features: One of Australia's most recognizable symbols, inaugurated by Queen Elizabeth II of England, the Opera House hosts more than three thousand different events every year.

Acknowledgments: UNESCO World Heritage Site since 2007.

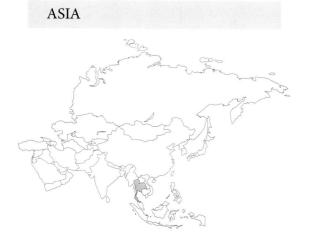

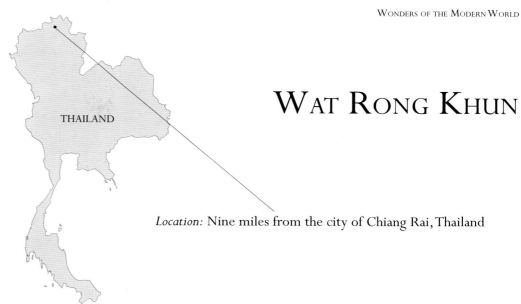

THAILAND

WAT RONG KHUN

Location: Nine miles from the city of Chiang Rai, Thailand

The White Temple of Chiang Rai is a construction that decidedly breaks the mold. From the distance, the structure beams in the sun for the brilliance of its intricate and complex decoration, covered with fragments of mirror mosaic that reflect the light and amplify the sense of absolute uniqueness of the building and its design. The work of the visionary painter Chalermchai Kositpipat, author of controversial creations, invokes the classic canons of Buddhist and Hindu temples but overturns these traditions in the details of strongly modern elements, such as the brilliant white color—so different from the color scheme of traditional temples—and the surreal, though thoroughly modern, sculptures. The walkway leading to the entrance of the temple forms a narrow path flanked by a forest of hands, both human and monstrous, emerging from the abyss on either side of the path: symbolizing the desires that entangle human beings. Two colossal statues serve as guardians to decide the fate of those who attempt passage. The roof of the temple is a thick forest of statues, bas-reliefs with curvilinear animals and dragons, depictions of the Buddha, and baroque elements of blinding white. Within, beside murals that depict the life story of the Buddha, paintings express unconventional approaches between the past and present, between tradition and popular culture, in a kitsch framework that resonates the contradictions of contemporaneity and invokes a new search for spirituality.

OPPOSITE: THE INTRICATE DECORATIONS OF THE WHITE TEMPLE OF CHIANG RAI, A CURIOUS FUSION OF THAI ART WITH BAROQUE ELEMENTS AND SINUOUS MODERN LINES, STAND OUT FOR THE BRIGHT WHITE OF THEIR REFLECTIVE SURFACES.
BELOW: DETAIL OF A STATUE THAT DECORATES THE WAT RONG KHUN TEMPLE, OF TRADITIONAL INSPIRATION BUT WITH MODERN LINES AND INNOVATIVE MATERIALS.
PP. 142-143: A VAST, CROWDED EXPANSE OF PLASTER HANDS, SYMBOL OF SOULS IN DISTRESS THAT ROAM THE UNDERWORLD, FLANKS THE ACCESS TO THE DAZZLING WAT RONG KHUN TEMPLE. THE ENTRANCE TO THE BUILDING SYMBOLIZES THE PURITY THAT CAN BE REACHED ONLY BY TRAVERSING THE DISHARMONY OF THE UNIVERSE WITHOUT BEING CORRUPTED.

Date: 1997, under construction.

Definition: Buddhist and Hindu temple constructed in plaster and mirror fragments, known as the White Temple.

Dimensions: Unspecified (under construction). The project involves the construction of other buildings for a total of nine structures, including a chapel for relics, a meditation hall, a monastery, and an art gallery.

Descriptive features: One of Thailand's most popular tourist attractions, the painter Chalermchai Kositpipat, author of the work, personally funded the construction of the temple, built on the base of an earlier building. The temple has often been criticized for being antithetical to tradition.

Acknowledgments: The artistic and cultural value is currently under discussion for its unconventionality.

BURJ KHALIFA

Location: Dubai, United Arab Emirates

UNITED ARAB EMIRATES

The Burj Khalifa, rising 2,217 feet overlooking Dubai's metropolis, is the tallest building in the world. The project, dedicated on the inauguration day of Sheikh Khalifa bin Zayed Al Nahyan, combines local cultural influences with state-of-the-art technology to meet the needs of a modern city within a desert climate. The mixed-use skyscraper contains offices, commercial spaces, housing units, and hotels (with interiors furnished by Armani). On the ground floor, the building is surrounded by green spaces, fountains with light displays, music, and pedestrian avenues of record dimension. Its design is inspired by the form of the *hymenocallis*, a traditional desert flower very common in Dubai, and its construction incorporates the characteristic patterns of Islamic architecture, inserted within an avant-garde context. Constructed in reinforced concrete and covered in glass, the tower consists of volumes sculpted around a central core, reducing the mass while increasing the height in the form of a spiral. In the near future, many designs across several states will undoubtedly endeavor to surpass the height of the Burj Khalifa: one of the major contenders (Al Burj), only thirty miles away, would reach a height of 3,280 feet, but the project remains pending because of current economic crises in the state.

OPPOSITE: VIEW OF THE BURJ KHALIFA SKYSCRAPER, ITS DESIGN INSPIRED BY THE SHAPE OF A CLASSIC DESERT FLOWER. BELOW: THE GLASS WINDOWS COVERING THE 2,217-FOOT BURJ KHALIFA GIVE TO THE SKYSCRAPER A MIRROR ASPECT, ELONGATING IMAGES INTO SINUOUS FORMS. PP. 146-147: THE BURJ KHALIFA STANDS OUT IN THE DUBAI SKYLINE, SURPASSING THE SURROUNDING BUILDINGS OF THE CITY'S FINANCIAL DISTRICT.

Date: 2010 (inauguration).

Definition: Skyscraper located in Dubai's main financial district.

Dimensions: 2,722.5 feet (including the spire) for a total of 163 floors and 3,702,785 square feet of walking area.

Descriptive features: The tallest building in the world, with the fastest elevators on the planet (60 feet per second). Between the 123rd and 124th floor there is an observation center with an outside terrace and a telescope with an LCD screen, offering real-time and recorded images of the panorama under various weather conditions. Outside the building, in an area of 2,960 square feet, is an elaborate system of fountains illuminated by 6,600 lights and 50 projectors, with jets of water that reach 500 feet high.

Acknowledgments: Officially designated the tallest building in the world by the Council on Tall Buildings and Urban Habitat in 2010.

WONDERS OF THE NATURAL WORLD

Though for the most part not present in the canonical list of wonders, nature's phenomena offer stunning expressions that can fill whole compendiums on the subject of wonder. Nature's extraordinary diversity of colors, forms, proportions, and scale—bearing the force of its most disruptive manifestations and the equally powerful silence of its stillness—creates unique wonders, witnessed before the reverential eyes of humankind, but wholly independent of human action. Rivers that cross continents, mountain ranges that touch the sky, multi-hued impenetrable forests, foreboding volcanoes, deserts of red land and even redder sunsets, effervescent shimmering waterfalls constitute the wonders of an Earth alive, vibrant, exuberant, at times hospitable and at times perilous to the human spectator: to see, experience, and live. In a collection of the most striking works of beauty, which in itself is, unfortunately, peremptorily selective, attention inevitably falls on macroscopic natural expressions. It is clear, however, that wonder beyond this small collection is sought and discovered in every corner of nature that surrounds us: from the highest waterfall to the intricate geometry of a spider's web, from the vastness of the desert to the flapping of a hummingbird's wings, great and small details testify to the perfection of a world that humankind inherits and, by that inheritance, assumes the responsibility of safeguarding.

The importance of land custodianship is crucial in this context. The beauty of the planet, which does not depend on humans' work, must in no way be obscured by the action of the latter. It is no coincidence that more attention is being devoted to natural wonders, with global initiatives led by UNESCO, which in its mission sets objectives toward biodiversity as an essential resource and reserve to be protected. Awareness of this necessity, however, is quite young, though a sign of a positive and proactive development of human responsibility toward an environment we have so much power to irrevocably alter, the great destructive potential of the modern world. The International Union for Conservation of Nature (IUCN), created in 1948 and working with UNESCO, today has 160 member states, 200 government agencies, 900 NGOs (nongovernmental organizations), and approximately 11,000 scientists from various parts of the world, the great constructive potential of the modern world. According to the IUCN, nearly 17,000 species are at risk of extinction, 99 percent of these due to human action. Destruction of natural habitats, introduction of species that alter ecosystems, invasive resource extraction, pollution, and poaching number only some of the behaviors that, for the wonders of the planet, merit serious pause for in-depth reconsideration and reflection.

The selection of a few beautiful works of nature among the staggering number of sceneries, environments, and ecosystems proves at the very least an arduous undertaking. The most effective approach, therefore, would endeavor variety, to offer a collection representative of a broader panorama that can embrace the greatest range of habitats and settings. From a perspective of contrasts, it is inevitable to first turn our gaze to the diversity between some of the most famous green areas and spectacular deserts. With this premise, attention is immediately rapt by the true green *lung* of the Earth: the Amazon Rainforest, one of the few pristine—uncharted—corners of the world that situates human beings squarely before primordial nature, a unique and vibrant habitat teeming with life. The astonishing wonder of the 2,124 million square miles covered with flora and fauna is a veritable planet in itself: the trees—constituting thousands of different species and more yet to be discovered—and vegetation form a nearly continuous thick and dense cover, rich in life and water. The colors, the smells, the sounds, and the sunlight through the canopy create the breathtaking atmosphere, home to animals of a thousand shapes and species and a few surviving indigenous peoples. However, this extraordinarily diverse ecosystem, so rich and so delicate, is highly at risk: the great wonder that produces the planet's largest forest must per force engender awareness, hope, and action that this unique area of the world is not compromised.

The Amazon Rainforest and other wondrous verdant expanses, each rich in its own character (California's Sequoia National Park, Germany's Black Forest, Banff National Park in the Canadian Rockies…), contrast the stunning desert lands, where flora gives way to enigmatic geologic formations, vast spaces where the gaze travels forever toward a far-distant horizon, desolate areas so incredibly hot or astoundingly cold, offering, each, their own pure wonder. Beyond the most iconic deserts (Sahara, Gobi, Kalahari), the mineral-rich desert of Atacama in northern Chile, the driest area in the world, absent of any oasis or water course, astonishes for its profound, almost palpable silence, a flat profile of earth where the sky directly encounters the barren land (a topography belonging to some distant planet). A giant hand thirty-six feet high emerges from the ground, work of Chilean artist Mario Irarrázabal, a symbol of aloneness and vulnerability, a monument to the emptiness of the desert and the darker side of humankind. The desert of salt in Uyuni, Bolivia, evokes similar sensations, by an immense area covered with layers of precious minerals, interrupted by holes in the land from which the underground water flows, creating brilliant reflections in a continuous play of mirrors.

Water is the great protagonist of some of the most spectacular expressions of nature: the fundamental element of life on Earth assumes the most varied and extreme forms within very different contexts of climate, latitude, and geology, and constitutes the lifeblood of many of the most beautiful landscapes on the planet. It is not possible to gaze indifferent at the immense ice colossal of the Perito Moreno, a massive solid wall in continuous motion, emerging majestically 200 feet above the level of the water: at times, serendipitously, a deep sound may be perceived, like thunder in the distance, when a huge block of ice wall detaches and collapses into the glacial lake with a resounding tremor. Quite a different aesthetic work, of fantastical and collected beauty, characterizes the translucent waters of Bermuda's Crystal Caves, so limpid one can see clear to the bottom of the crystalline pools, even 66 feet deep. Above the blue of the water, white stalactites drip from the cave ceiling as stalagmites rise from the cave floor, reaching to the center of the cave, which descends 200 feet. Among the other wonders, extraordinary lakes and rivers, vast and long and of intense colors, sculpt the landscape in an immense planetary hydraulic network. Beyond the river giants, such as the Nile and the Amazon—primordial arteries of the planet in length and breadth—wonders also arise in unexpected natural exhibitions, where water assumes curious and varied colors. The incredible pink of Lake Hillier in Australia and the iridescent and smoky tones of the Grand Prismatic Spring in Yellowstone Park may seem

divergent in the surrounding greenery, but they stand out in a strange harmony. The water turns in its most disruptive expressions in some of the most famous and admired natural wonders of the planet: the thunderous liquid wall of Victoria Falls, the spontaneous rainbows materializing in the spray and mist of Iguaçu Falls, and the colorfully illuminated uproar of Niagara Falls at night. Earth, as well as water, mold some of the most amazing landscapes of the planet: record mountain chains, curious geologic conformations, active volcanoes, and stunningly polychromatic stone often characterize inaccessible and inhospitable worlds, where wonder emerges in the presence of the imposing colossus of nature. The variety of such expressions is fascinating, from the white Himalayan peaks, rich in epithets (*roof of the world*, *snow dwelling*) for its undeniable uniqueness, to the orange profile of Uluru, solitary massif of the Australian Outback, with its blunt lines, changeable at every sunset. For a change of scenery, a journey might begin at the curving, streaking stratifications of the Grand Canyon, continue to the vertical with the natural pinnacles of Monument Valley, and conclude on the flat square peak of Table Mountain (at the southernmost tip of Africa). For a wonder of inspired tranquility, Mount Fuji emerges, custodian of Japan, framed in clouds and cherry blossoms that bathe its slopes. For a more disquieted inspiration, Etna, the "nervous" volcano of

the poet Pindar, is rich in diverse environments (forest, desert, snow) in the heart of the Mediterranean, a UNESCO World Heritage Site since 2013. A panorama of the most striking natural wonders of the world cannot exclude other fascinating phenomena that distinguish the planet. The diversity of colors and life forms of the coral reefs throughout the tropical oceans profoundly enchants: among the coral and algae, that feed on light traversing translucent waters, life thrives in countless species of fish, turtles, and sharks. The Australian Great Barrier Reef, a surface of nearly 134 square miles, is the largest living structure on Earth. Still other climates characterize the lands that lie below the evanescent lights of the Aurora Borealis (Northern Lights) and Aurora Australis (Southern Lights), at the earth's poles. The Aurorae range of colors and shapes, of harmonious beauty, projects the sensation of wonder even outside the physicality of the planet itself, in a reality suspended between earth and sky.

GREAT BARRIER REEF

AUSTRALIA

Location: Off the northeast coast of Australia

During the voyage of navigator Captain James Cook around the Pacific Islands, the captain's ship ran aground on what was later discovered to be the world's largest coral reef. The explorer had to throw a substantial load of his cargo overboard in order to lighten the ship and reach deeper waters. The natural barrier off the coast of Australia is the result of fifteen thousand years of coral growth: the progressive rise of the sea caused the proliferation of coral on the flooded lands, rooting and stratifying across millennia on the remains of ancient banks to finally reach sea level. The Great Barrier Reef is an unforgettable marvel: among the limestone branches the translucent sea teems with life, home to more than 1,500 species of fish, 400 species of coral, more than 30 species of whales and dolphins, and numerous endemic and protected species, creating an ecosystem of diversity and colors unique in the world. To safeguard this wondrous reality, the Great Barrier Reef Marine Park was created off the coast of Queensland, establishing a protected area for sustainable resource management.

OPPOSITE AND BELOW: THE INCREDIBLE COLORS OF THE AUSTRALIAN BARRIER REEF, ONE OF THE MOST COLORFUL AND BIODIVERSE NATURAL WONDERS OF THE WORLD.
PP. 158-159: AERIAL VIEW OF THE GREAT BARRIER REEF IN QUEENSLAND, AUSTRALIA.

Definition: The world's largest coral reef.

Dimensions: 1,430 miles of barrier for an area of approximately 133,000 square miles.

Descriptive features: Environment of extraordinary biodiversity, consisting of numerous coral reefs alongside each other (approximately 3,000) and islets (nearly 1,000).

Acknowledgments: UNESCO World Heritage Site since 1981.

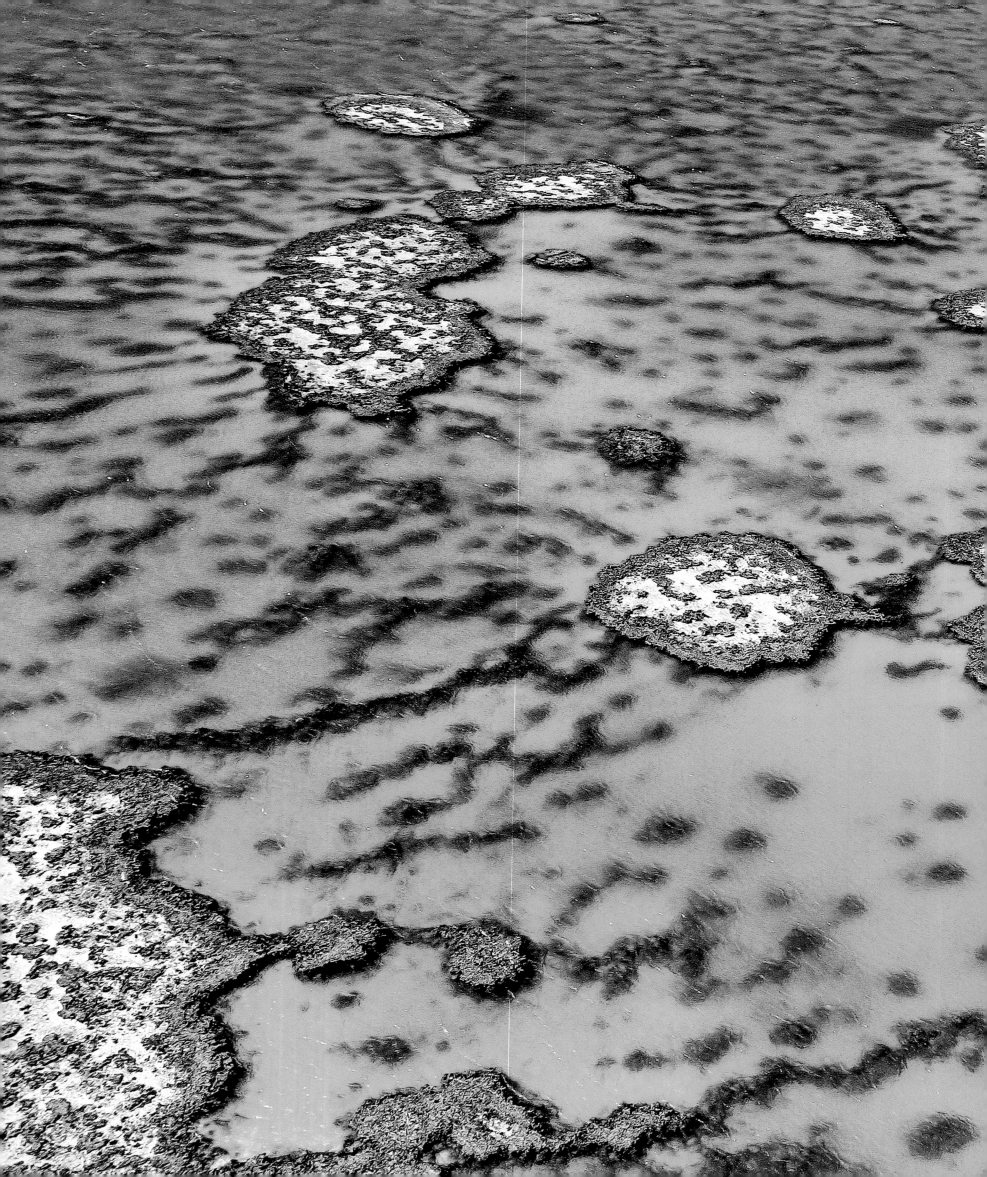

ULURU (AYERS ROCK)

AUSTRALIA

Location: 280 miles southwest of
Alice Springs, Australia

The Uluru Massif rises like a sentinel in the flat landscape characteristic of the Australian Outback. At sunset, the minerals that compose the massif reflect a red light rendering the stone iridescent, elucidating why the Aborigine people believe this imposing monolith heavily anchored in the earth is sacred. The myths of *Dreamtime*, before the arrival of humankind, correlate the corrosive phenomena on the surface of Uluru with the presence of ancestral and supernatural beings, depicted in cave paintings, which enrich the colorful stone. Today Uluru teems with visitors, referred to by the locals, the Pitjantjatjara, as *minga tjuta*, "ants," because they appear so small before the mammoth walls of this monolith intense in colors that change every hour of the day.

OPPOSITE AND BELOW: THE UNMISTAKABLE REDDISH PROFILE OF AYERS ROCK, *DISCOVERED* BY WILLIAM GOSSE IN 1873 AND DEDICATED TO THE PRIME MINISTER AT THE TIME, HENRY AYERS.

Definition: Rock massif, reddish-orange in color.

Dimensions: 2.2 miles long x 1.5 miles wide, rising to an altitude of 1,148 feet.

Descriptive features: Monolith extending into the earth for several miles, its position and conformation causing it to continually change color depending on the light. According to Aborigine belief, the rock carries the signs of passage of the ancestral beings belonging to a mythical past.

Acknowledgments: The Uluru-Kata Tjuta National Park has been listed a UNESCO World Heritage Site since 1987.

SEQUOIA NATIONAL PARK

UNITED STATES

Location: Sierra Nevada, California, United States

Sequoia National Park, united with Kings Canyon Park in 1984, garners many records. The dimensions of the trees within its forest are impressive and for no small reason called *giant*: the height and diameter of the sequoia seem to belong to a scale far out of the ordinary. The General Sherman is the emblem of the park, one of the world's tallest specimens, reaching almost 275 feet, with a base diameter over 36 feet, making it, by volume, the largest known living single stem tree on the planet. The extraordinary nature of this and other specimens of the park has led UNESCO to designate the site a *biosphere reserve*, an area of land or sea identified by the member states to be protected and managed to balance conservation of biodiversity and sustainable use.

OPPOSITE: THE MASSIVE TRUNK OF THE GIANT SEQUOIA, NAMED GENERAL SHERMAN IN HONOR OF THE FAMOUS AMERICAN CIVIL WAR GENERAL. FROM DENDROLOGICAL ANALYSIS, THE GENERAL SHERMAN COULD BE FROM 2,300 TO 2,700 YEARS OLD.
BELOW: A WALK IN SEQUOIA NATIONAL PARK OFFERS A CAPTIVATING JOURNEY THROUGH SOME OF THE MOST WONDROUS LIVING ORGANISMS ON THE PLANET.

Definition: National park managed by the US National Park Service.

Dimensions: 631 square miles.

Descriptive features: The park is home to the General Sherman, the largest tree in the world, and Mount Whitney, the tallest mountain in the United States; in the giant sequoia forest exist five of the ten largest trees in the world.

Acknowledgments: Designated a biosphere reserve by UNESCO since 1976.

GRAND PRISMATIC SPRING

UNITED STATES

Location: Yellowstone National Park, Wyoming, United States

In no other location in the world is a concentration of hot springs equal to that of Yellowstone Park, a result of intense volcanic activity and tectonic plate movements that led to the formation of the Central Rocky Mountains. Among the most famous and spectacular springs is the Grand Prismatic Spring, which offers a spectacle of rare beauty. The largest hot spring in the United States, the Grand Prismatic forms with its outflow of extremely hot water an expansive lake of vibrant and fluorescent colors, acquiring its varied tints from pigmented thermophile (heat-loving) bacteria that thrive in the spring waters, ranging from green to red depending on temperature and season—blue and dark green in winter, yellow and orange in summer—forming a sort of scalding liquid rainbow. A walkway allows visitors to approach the edge of the spring to observe the colorful play up close; an aerial view proves even more spectacular, as the lake stands out a unique and unusual spot of color surrounded by the greenery of the park.

OPPOSITE, BELOW, AND PP. 166-167: THE COLORS OF THE GRAND PRISMATIC SPRING CREATE BREATHTAKING EFFECTS. THE PROFUNDITY OF COLOR IN THE LAKE'S MICROBIAL NETWORK DEPENDS ON THE CHLOROPHYLL, CAROTENOIDS, AND WATER TEMPERATURE. A WALKWAY LEADS VISITORS THROUGH FIREHOLE RIVER, ALONG THE BOILING BANKS OF THE LAKE.

Definition: Thermal spring characterized by brilliant colors.

Dimensions: 820 x 1,246 feet.

Descriptive Features: The largest thermal spring in the United States and the third-largest in the world, characterized by unusual and varied coloration.

Acknowledgments: Yellowstone Park has been listed a UNESCO World Heritage Site since 1978.

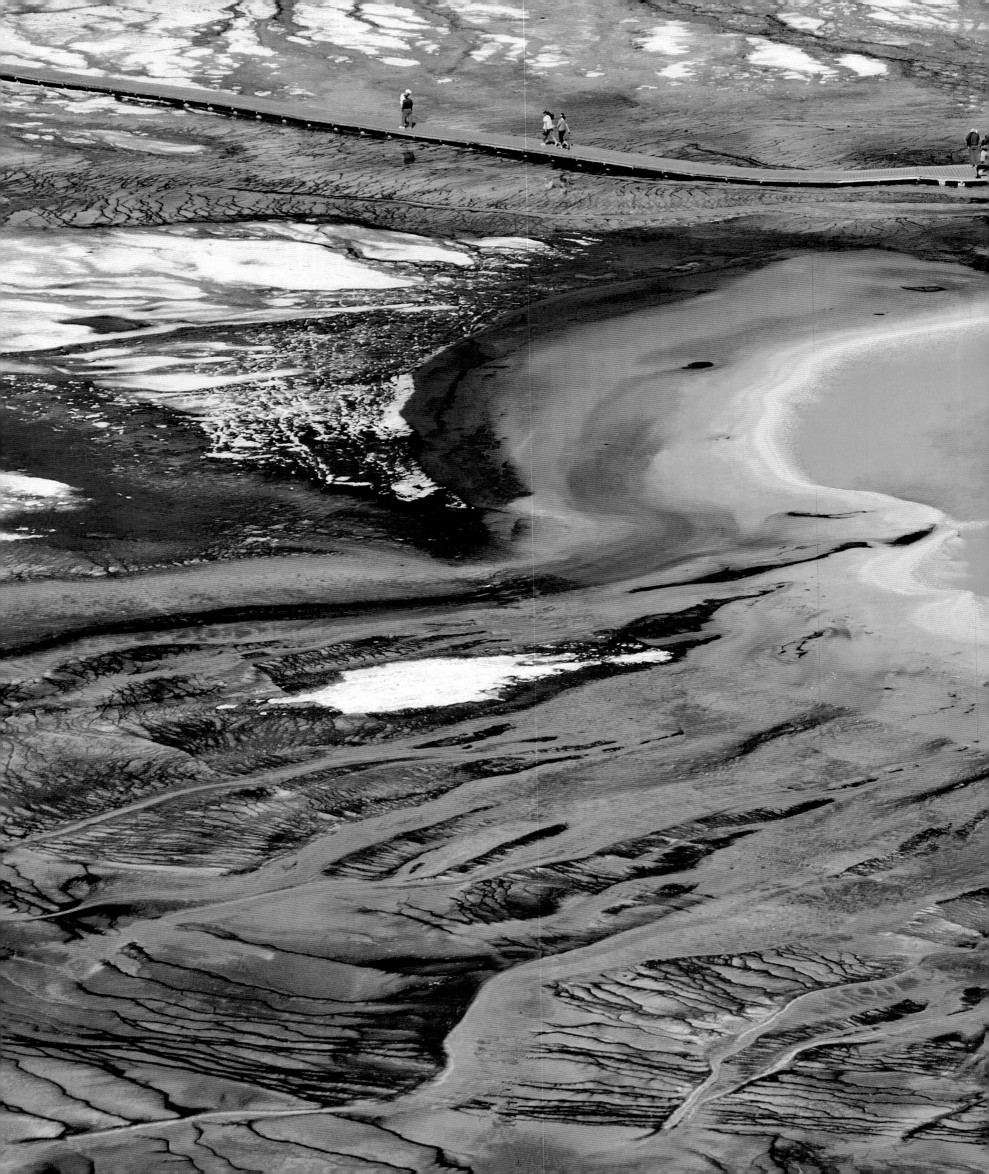

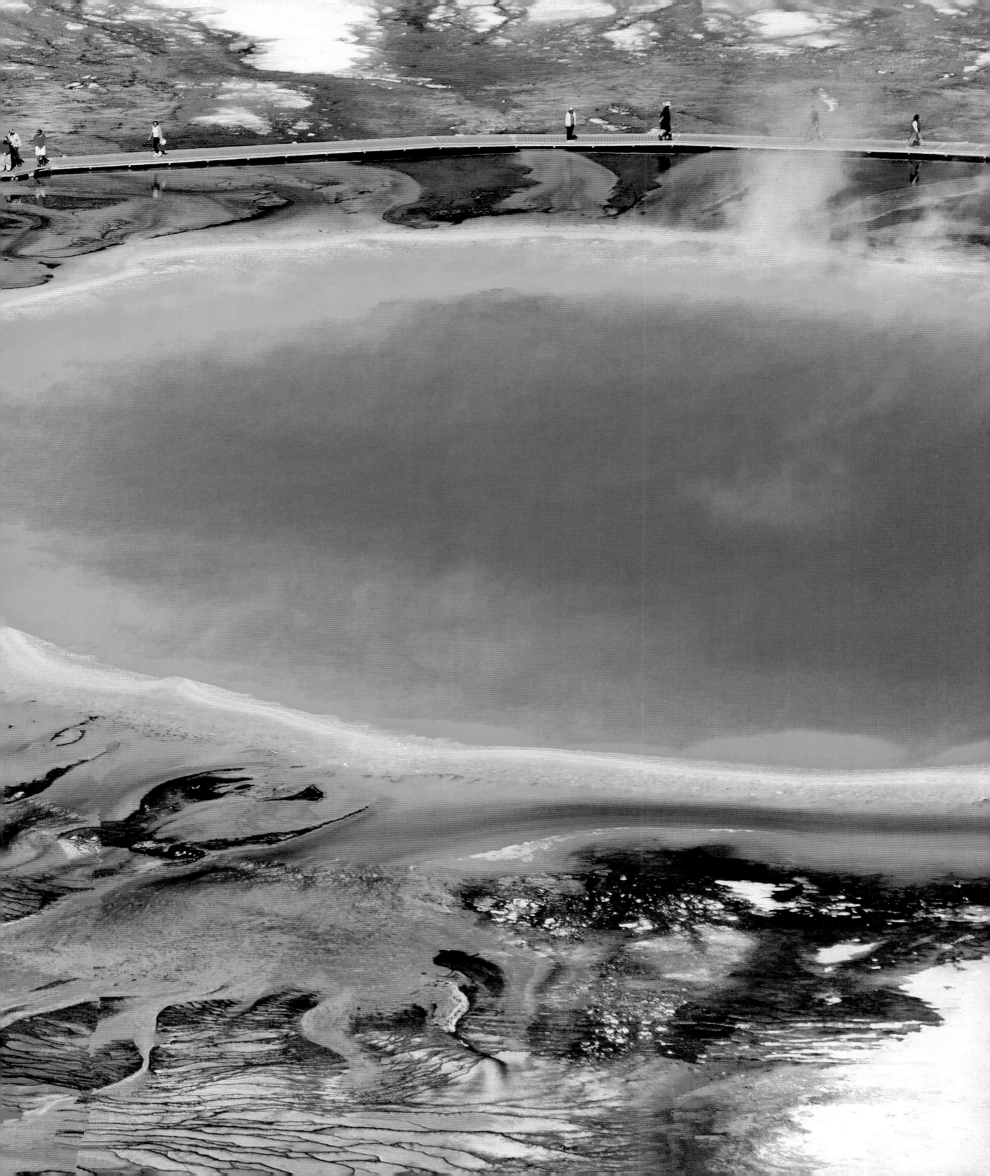

GRAND CANYON

UNITED STATES

Location: Northern Arizona, United States

The Grand Canyon is one of the most extensive and impressive geological marvels on the planet. Its vastness is astonishing, offering one of the most visually powerful landscapes in the world with its deep gorges, labyrinthine topography, and the multicolored geologic stratifications that can be read along its precipitous walls. Formed by over six million years of geologic activity and the erosion caused by the Colorado River, the details of its orogenesis remain in part a mystery. The majestic beauty of its geologic formations is well known to visitors, outdoor enthusiasts, and adventurers from all over the world, who discover in the Grand Canyon spectacular landscapes and the opportunity to test one's mettle and sense of adventure. One such adventurer in 2013, aerialist Nik Wallenda, walked across the canyon on a tightrope without a safety net.

OPPOSITE: VIEW OF THE GRAND CANYON FROM THE FAMOUS SCENIC LOOKOUT OF TOROWEAP POINT, ALSO KNOWN AS TUWEEP. BELOW: HORSESHOE BEND IS ONE OF THE MOST PHOTOGRAPHED AREAS OF THE COLORADO RIVER, LOCATED JUST NORTH OF THE GRAND CANYON. THE GLASS GREEN OF THE RIVER'S WATER CONTRASTS WITH THE INTENSE AND LUMINOUS COLORS OF THE REDDISH ROCK.
PP. 170-171: VIEW OF THE COLORADO RIVER AT GLEN CANYON, NORTH OF THE FAMOUS GRAND CANYON.

Definition: Rocky gorge created by the Colorado River, an expression of intense geologic activity.

Dimensions: Length approximately 277 river miles, average depth one mile, minimum expanse rim to rim 1,650 feet, maximum expanse rim to rim 18 miles.

Descriptive features: Because of the Colorado River's excavation of the canyon, more than two billion years of Earth's history come to light and can be read along the canyon's stratified walls; there is still no complete authoritative account of the canyon's formation. The Grand Canyon is well visible from Space, 186 miles above the Earth's surface at the International Space Station.

Acknowledgments: Grand Canyon National Park has been listed a UNESCO World Heritage Site since 1979.

SOUTH AMERICA

THE AMAZON FOREST

Location: Brazil, Colombia, Venezuela, Guyana, Bolivia, Peru, Ecuador (South America)
(● Area Covered by the Amazon Forest)

South America is extensively covered by an incredible green expanse, considered the Earth's *lung*: the Amazon Forest. Along the course of the Amazon River a tropical habitat flourishes with extraordinary biodiversity: millions of animal and plant species thrive and proliferate in the humid, rainy environment of the equatorial forest, creating a unique biome for the world. The life-giving artery that traverses the forest is the Amazon River, which flows into the Atlantic Ocean at its terminus, a course that nourishes with its exceptional waters the fauna and flora extended from its shores: The Amazon basin is the largest freshwater reserve on the planet. Nevertheless, the incredibly dense concentration of animal and plant species renders the Amazon one of the least human-populated zones on the planet, fewer than one inhabitant per square mile. Tribes of Indigenous peoples live in the Amazon but occupy increasingly limited portions of land.

OPPOSITE AND BELOW: THE AMAZON RIVER FEEDS THE IMMENSE RAINFOREST THAT EXTENDS OVER A SURFACE AREA EQUAL TO ALMOST 42 PERCENT OF THE SURFACE AREA OF EUROPE.
P. 174: PARROTS ARE THE MOST CHARACTERISTIC BIRDS OF THE AMAZON. AMONG THE MOST NOTABLE SPECIES, THE *ARA ARARAUNA* AND THE *ARA MACAO*.
P. 175: THE RED-EYED TREE FROG IS AN ICON OF THE RAINFOREST, RANGING IN BRIGHT COLORS OF GREEN, BLUE, AND YELLOW.

Definition: Tropical rainforest along the Amazon River.

Dimensions: 2,124 million square miles.

Descriptive features: The Amazon forms the largest area of forest in the world and one of the richest in biodiversity, traversed by the longest river in the world (4,311 miles).

Acknowledgments: The Central Amazon Conservation Complex has been listed a UNESCO World Heritage Site since 2000.

ARGENTINA

PERITO MORENO GLACIER

Location: Santa Cruz Province, Patagonia, Argentina

The wonder the Perito Moreno Glacier offers is stirring: an ice wall more than two hundred feet high looms over the water of Lake Argentino—one of the principal glacial lakes in Los Glaciares National Park—advancing several feet every day. The landscape of Los Glaciares offers an extraordinary visual impact of blue-white expanse embraced by mountains, accompanied by the thunderous sound of ice blocks breaking free from the glacier and collapsing into water, in some rare cases with veritable explosions of enormous ice masses. Amplifying its presence, the imposing glacier contrasts with the often-overcast sky and the beautiful natural setting of snow-stepped mountains characteristic of the Patagonian landscape, the southern extremity of South America.

OPPOSITE, BELOW AND PP. 178-179: VIEWS OF THE PERITO MORENO GLACIAL WALL, WHICH ASSUMES SHADES OF GREEN OR BLUE DEPENDING ON THE LIGHT.

Definition: Large glacier on Lake Argentino, the most important attraction in Los Glaciares National Park.

Dimensions: Surface area approximately 97 square miles, length 19 miles, height 200 feet.

Descriptive features: The third-largest freshwater reserve in the world, a moving glacier advancing on average 6 feet a day.

Acknowledgments: Los Glaciares National Park has been listed a UNESCO World Heritage Site since 1981.

IGUAÇU FALLS

Location: On the border between Misiónes (Argentina) and Paraná (Brazil)

The verdant Iguaçu National Park contains one of the most famous and admired waterfalls in the world. The Iguaçu River is divided into nearly three hundred discrete falls, which descend with numerous leaps the basalt terraces beneath. During the rainy season, water draws down from the precipice at 448,496 cubic feet per second: a cloud of mist creates a climate of high humidity, perfect for the growth of the lush vegetation that characterizes the park. The humidity feeds the tropical rainforest along the course of the river, including typical ferns and lianas and endemic animal species, such as the giant anteater and the harpy eagle.

OPPOSITE: AMONG THE RUSHING CASCADES OF THE IGUAÇU FALLS, IT IS NOT RARE TO SEE SUDDEN RAINBOWS SPONTANEOUSLY APPEAR, CAUSED BY LIGHT PASSING THROUGH THE MIST. BELOW AND PP. 182-183: LUSH VEGETATION CHARACTERIZES THE LANDSCAPE SURROUNDING IGUAÇU FALLS. A WALK INSIDE THE NATIONAL PARK BETWEEN ARGENTINA AND BRAZIL OFFERS A CONTINUOUS DISCOVERY OF AN ECOSYSTEM UNIQUE IN THE WORLD.

Definition: Waterfalls of the Iguaçu River between Argentina and Brazil, in Iguaçu National Park.

Dimensions: Maximum cascade 263 feet, width 1.7 miles.

Descriptive features: One of the most famous and striking waterfall systems in the world; the gorge *Garganta del Diablo* measures 492 feet deep and marks the border between the two countries.

Acknowledgments: Iguaçu National Park has been listed a World Heritage Site on the Argentine side since 1984 and on the Brazilian side since 1986.

ATACAMA DESERT

CHILE

Location: Atacama Region and Arica and Parinacota Region, Chile

About five hundred miles north of Santiago, in northern Chile, a barren and arid land stretches out, unique and captivating: the Atacama Desert. Notwithstanding the complete absence of any oasis and signs of life—a distinction of the land that scientists explore to understand how life might be possible on the planet Mars—the desert offers a curious and captivating landscape and, within the profound silence that surrounds it, a perspective of earth that is inimitable and fascinating. The peaks of the Andes and the Cordillera de la Costa rise, framing the desert in variegated scenery: salt plains, copper mines, archaeological sites, beaches, and gentle slopes populated by llamas and alpaca surround the arid and barren expanse. Installed in 1992, in the middle of the desert, the sculpture of a giant hand appears to emerge directly from the land, work of Mario Irarrázabal, symbolizing human vulnerability before the surrounding emptiness.

OPPOSITE: EROSION OF THE ROCK CAUSED BY THE DRY WINDS CREATES UNIQUE AND SOLITARY PROFILES IN THE HEART OF THE ATACAMA DESERT.
BELOW: THE VALLEY OF THE MOON IN THE ATACAMA DESERT COMPOSES A WONDROUS ARRAY OF FORMS AND COLORS, REMINISCENT OF THE DESOLATION OF A LUNAR LANDSCAPE.
PP. 186-187: VIEW OF THE EL TATIO VALLEY OF GEYSERS, CONTAINING MORE THAN EIGHTY ACTIVE GEYSERS.

Definition: Chilean rocky desert between the Andes and the Cordillera along the Pacific coastline.

Dimensions: 40,540 square miles.

Descriptive features: The Atacama is the most arid and barren desert in the world, characterized by the complete absence of any oasis; the mineral wealth of the desert renders it a contested territory. The area of San Pedro de Atacama was inhabited in the Paleolithic Era.

OPPOSITE: THE ROCK FORMATIONS OF THE
ATACAMA ARE SURROUNDED BY THE ANDES
AND COASTAL MOUNTAINS, WHICH PROTECT
THE DESERT FROM HUMIDITY AND MAKE THE
AREA THE MOST ARID IN THE WORLD.

SALAR DE UYUNI

BOLIVIA

Location: Environs of the city of Uyuni, Bolivia

The salt desert in Uyuni offers an unforgettable landscape: over 3,860 square miles covered in a flat salt crust, on average three feet thick. When the surface is dry, saline transforms the landscape into an expanse of blinding white, covered by an exceptional reserve of brine rich in lithium (50–70 percent of the world's lithium reserves). Water comes to the land in the form of rain and underground courses flowing from holes in the terrain, called *Ojos de Salar* ("Eyes of the Salt"), at one time feared because they *swallowed* caravans.

When the surface is covered in water, the spectacle is amazing: the land mirrors the sky in detailed precision, the horizon vanishing as heaven and earth combine into a single landscape.

OPPOSITE: HEAPS OF SALT IN THE UYUNI SALT PANS, IN THE SOUTHERN ANDEAN PLATEAU OF BOLIVIA. APPROXIMATELY 25,000 TONS OF SALT ARE EXTRACTED ANNUALLY.
BELOW AND PP. 192-193: THE PLAY OF REFLECTIONS BETWEEN THE CLOUDS, THE WATER, AND THE PURE WHITE SALT IS ONE OF THE MAJOR ATTRACTIONS OF THE UYUNI SALT PANS, A UNIQUE PLACE IN THE WORLD, WITH A LANDSCAPE SUSPENDED BETWEEN HEAVEN AND EARTH.

Definition: Salt desert in the southern Andean tableland, Bolivia.

Dimensions: 4,085 square miles, elevation 12,025 feet.

Descriptive features: The largest salt expanse in the world, estimated to contain 10 billion tons of salt, representing approximately one half of the lithium reserves on the planet.

Acknowledgments: Under assessment by UNESCO.

EGYPT

SUDAN

SOUTH SUDAN

UGANDA

RUANDA

BURUNDI

CONGO

ETHIOPIA

KENYA

TANZANIA

NILE RIVER

Location: Egypt, Sudan, South Sudan, Ethiopia, Kenya, Tanzania, Uganda, Congo

The extraordinariness of the Nile River is undeniable. Considered for centuries the longest river in the world—today sharing that designation with the Amazon River—and one of the largest on the planet for the volume of its basin, the Nile is famous for the civilization that settled, endured, and forged several empires on its banks beginning more than five thousand years ago. The Ancient Egyptians discovered in the fertility of the Nile wetlands, unexpected in a desert region, the prime engine for the emergence of an advanced and complex urban civilization. Believed a sacred river for its flood cycle that brought vast and rich seasonal harvests, the Nile also functioned as a strategic and extensive mode of transportation, from the wood and papyrus boats of the Old Kingdom of the past to the cruise ships of the modern era, transporting visitors to discover the innumerable archaeological sites along the river's course. The main artery of North Africa, the Nile begins in the heart of the African continent, at Lake Victoria, and crosses several countries before flowing into the Mediterranean Sea, forming a vast delta with an overall surface area of approximately 9,266 square miles.

OPPOSITE: NILE LANDSCAPE AT LUXOR, EGYPT. BOATS AND BARGES HAVE NAVIGATED THE RIVER SINCE ANCIENT TIMES.
BELOW: THE NILE IS THE TRUE ARTERY THAT NOURISHED AND GAVE LIFE TO THE ANCIENT EGYPTIAN CIVILIZATION, VESTIGES OF WHICH LEAVE THEIR TESTIMONY ALONG THE BANKS OF THE RIVER.
PP. 196-197: THE FERTILE NILE VALLEY, WITH ITS CULTIVATIONS OF WHEAT, SUGAR CANE, AND OTHER CROPS, CONTRASTS WITH THE DESERT LANDSCAPE CHARACTERISTIC OF THE EGYPTIAN TERRAIN.

Definition: African river flowing into a vast delta into the Mediterranean Sea.

Dimensions: Length 4,258 miles, average flow rate 99,940 cubic feet per second.

Descriptive features: The Nile shares the record with the Amazon River as the longest river on the planet, its basin covering approximately 10 percent of the surface area of Africa; the river was the driving force for the birth of the Egyptian civilization.

Acknowledgments: Numerous UNESCO World Heritage Sites are located along the Nile's course.

VICTORIA FALLS

Location: Border between Zambia and Zimbabwe, Africa

ZAMBIA

ZIMBABWE

When David Livingstone visited the waterfalls in 1855 and named them in honor of the queen of England at the time, he most likely did not imagine that only a century and half later the site would become part of two national parks and one of Africa's most beloved visitor attractions. The thunderous cascade of water and spray of such great intensity and force plummeting through a series of awe-inspiring gorges on the Zambezi River offers the modern visitor the same experience as Livingstone when he first beheld the *Mosi-oa-Tunya* (from the local language, "Smoke that Thunders"). The great cascades of water, falling hundreds of feet with a thunderous sound, generate clouds of mist and spray that can rise to five thousand feet in the air, enveloping the area in a perennial mist and producing spontaneous rainbows. Numerous islets divide a cascade into different branches, creating a spectacle of awe-inspiring beauty.

OPPOSITE, BELOW, AND PP. 200-201: AERIAL AND FRONTAL VIEWS OF VICTORIA FALLS. THE ZAMBEZI, FOLLOWING A REMARKABLE CASCADE OF MORE THAN FOUR HUNDRED FEET, FLOWS BETWEEN DEEP AND TORTUOUS GORGES. ABOVE, THE CAPE CONGO RAILWAY LINE CROSSES A VERTIGINOUS BRIDGE.

Definition: Waterfalls of the Zambezi River.

Dimensions: Height 420 feet, maximum cascade 354 feet, maximum width one mile.

Descriptive features: One of the most famous and spectacular waterfalls in the world, offering panoramas of awe-inspiring beauty from its narrow gorge.

Acknowledgments: UNESCO World Heritage Site since 1989.

TABLE MOUNTAIN

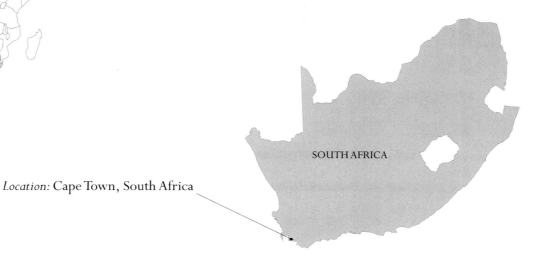

SOUTH AFRICA

Location: Cape Town, South Africa

The mountain with a summit flat like a tabletop is the landmark of Cape Town and a beloved visitor attraction. An integral part of the city, Table Mountain overlooks the populated urban center, offering a panoramic view from above. The highest point of the mountain is Maclear's Beacon, named in honor of the astronomer Thomas Maclear, who in the nineteenth century used the summit as the basis for a series of calculations and observations designed to define the size and shape of the Earth. The mountain, with its three-mile façade facing the city, is a distinctly characteristic sight, and equally characteristic is the windy climate and blanket of clouds that surround the summit, due to humidity from the east.

OPPOSITE AND BELOW: THE IMPOSING TABLE MOUNTAIN, WITH ITS UNMISTAKABLE PROFILE, EMERGES NEAR CAPE TOWN.

Definition: Flat-topped mountain, part of a sandstone mountain range, overlooking Cape Town.

Elevation: 33,000 feet.

Descriptive features: The mountain summit is flat, like a tabletop, and the clouds that cover it called, consequently, *tablecloths.* A *Cable Car* transports visitors up the mountain, which rotates to allow passengers a complete view of the landscape.

Acknowledgments: Table Mountain National Park has been listed a UNESCO World Heritage Site since 2004 (under the name "Cape Floral Region Protected Areas," which includes other sites in the area).

HIMALAYAS

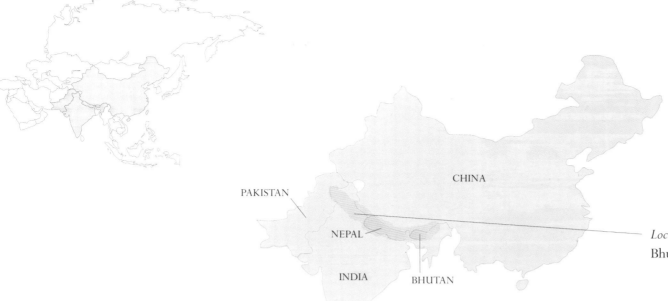

Location: India, Nepal, Pakistan, China, Bhutan (● Himalayan Mountain Range)

The Himalayan mountain range is one of the most legendary sites in the world for its incredible expanse and spectacular majesty. Crossing five countries, the Himalayas include the fourteen *Eight-Thousander*s, mountains with elevations greater than 8,000 meters (26,247 feet), including Everest and K2. The view of the extraordinary snowy peaks evokes awe, and it is not hard to imagine why the summits of the *roof of the world* have always embodied the sacred: among the clouds and at altitudes inhospitable to humans, only divinities may dwell. Sagarmatha National Park, at the base of Mount Everest, offers breathtaking panoramas within a rugged landscape and severe habitat, home to indigenous animals (such as snow leopards) and the solitary Sherpas.

OPPOSITE: THE PERENNIAL SNOWS OF THE HIMALAYAS OFFER A SPECTACLE OF INCREDIBLE BEAUTY.
BELOW: PROFILE OF MOUNT MANASLU, IN NEPAL, THE EIGHTH-HIGHEST MOUNTAIN IN THE WORLD. THE WORD *MANASLU* DERIVES FROM *MANASA*, "MOUNTAIN OF THE SOUL."
PP. 206-207: IN THE WESTERN PART OF THE MOUNTAIN RANGE, THE KARAKORUM IS HOME TO VARIOUS PEAKS MORE THAN 26,000 FEET HIGH (INCLUDING MOUNT EVEREST) AND GIANT GLACIERS.

Definition: Central and South Asian mountain range.

Dimensions: Length 1,500 miles; highest peak (Everest), elevation 29,029 feet.

Descriptive features: Called the *Roof of the World* and *Dwelling of Snow*, the Himalayas contain the highest mountain summits on the planet.

Acknowledgments: Sagarmatha National Park, at the base of Mount Everest, has been listed a UNESCO World Heritage Site since 1979.

MOUNT FUJI

JAPAN

Location: Shizuoka and Yamanashi Prefectures, Chubu region, Japan

Japan's unmistakable symbol and icon, the snowy summit of Mount Fuji stands out in countless photographic and pictorial representations, modern and traditional. Its peak is observable from many parts of central Japan, from Tokyo itself, approximately eighty miles away. The volcano has for centuries been revered as a divinity, with a sense of admiration and reverence in respect to its continuous volcanic activity. Fuji, in fact, remained an active volcano until 1706. Even today the high mountain assumes an elevated sense: considered one of the three sacred mountains of the country, with Mount Tateyama and Mount Hakusan. A large number of temples populate the slopes of Mount Fuji, and more than one hundred thousand people per year climb its symmetrical cone, to the borders of the eight jagged crests that comprise its crater.

OPPOSITE: ENCHANTING VIEW OF MOUNT FUJI, SYMBOL OF JAPAN AND SACRED SHINTO MOUNTAIN.
BELOW: AERIAL VIEW OF THE FUJI CRATER. THE SUMMIT IS COVERED IN SNOW TEN MONTHS OUT OF THE YEAR.
PP. 210-211: THE CHUREITO PAGODA, IN FUJIYOSHIDA, AGAINST THE BACKDROP OF MOUNT FUJI.

Definition: Composite (conical) volcano in Fuji-Hakone-Izu National Park.

Height: 12,388 feet above sea level.

Descriptive features: The highest mountain in Japan, a symbol of the country and a sacred Shinto location.

Acknowledgments: UNESCO World Heritage Site since 2013.

MOUNT ETNA

ITALY

Location: Province of Catania, Sicily, Italy

The volcanic complex of Etna, on the eastern coast of Sicily, is one of the most significant in Europe for its height and continuous activity. Its profile is the symbol of ancient *Trinacria* ("Sicily"). Characterized by a variety of remarkable environments, Etna's surface, according to Greek and Roman mythology and popular beliefs from Antiquity, was populated by gods and giants, responsible for the continuous eruptions of lava. Etna's eruptions from the central and side craters produce fascinating colors, reaching heights of hundreds of feet above sea level. The most recent eruptions began in 2011 with a series of lava fountains, an episode that lasted until the end of 2013. Etna remains one of the most active volcanoes in the world and, with a diameter of 28 miles, is one of the largest on the planet.

OPPOSITE: THE YELLOW IN THE BARREN LANDSCAPE OF ETNA'S CRATER IS DUE TO THE CONCENTRATIONS OF SULFUR.
BELOW: ETNA DURING AN ERUPTION.

Definition: Composite (conical) volcano characterized mainly by rare explosive lava flows characteristic of shield volcanoes.

Elevation: 11,000 feet.

Descriptive features: The highest active volcano in Europe.

Acknowledgments: UNESCO World Heritage Site since 2013.

WHEN NATURE ENCOUNTERS HUMANKIND

The relationship between humans and nature has time and again proved rather complex. From the astonishment of the first people before the inexplicable phenomena of the earth and sky to the modern metropolises in which urbanization has molded the ground to its will, the interaction between the two most influential forces on the planet rests at the core of human history. The boundaries of this mutual influence remain elusive, even erratic at times, with one reality affecting the other, not always to the highest virtue. Too often the contemporary, industrialized world has caused, to varying degrees, significant alteration to the ecosystem through deforestation, pollution, over-exploitation of non-renewable resources, and many other behaviors endangering the health and vitality of the land. In turn, nature not infrequently has prostrated humans with undeniable, at times devastating, force: earthquakes, floods, volcanic eruptions remind time and again of the fragile balance that lies at the heart of the multi-faceted relationship between the Earth and its inhabitants.

Within a collection of *wonders* of the planet, the fascinating results of this interaction cannot go unrecognized. In fact, many of the works of beauty divided between *natural* and *human* do not entirely adhere to the categorization: the two categories derive from each other, amplifying, from the interaction, the extraordinary. The Great Pyramid could not be the wonder it is without the context of the flat desert landscape, the topography from which it emerges, soaring to the sky in our gaze, and acquires its redolent color. Christ the Redeemer would not have the same invocative force if not overlooking all the city of Rio de Janeiro and the sea from atop the Corcovado. In turn, Mount Fuji, a natural wonder, draws from the solitary temples that adorn it the inspired atmosphere of the slopes. Likewise, Uluru accompanies its spontaneous beauty with the enchantment of the aboriginal legends evoked on its ancient rock.

In some cases, the *wonder* of this virtuous interaction between human and nature is more intentional, when an emotion is willingly sought to create a majestic work using the inherent natural beauty of a place. Other times, harmony springs spontaneously, in biophilic landscapes where human and nature converse constructively, giving life to forms both curious and unique.

The extraordinary profiles in the granite of Mount Rushmore, South Dakota, offer a majestic human opera that incorporates the significance of the Black Hills and at the same time converses with the surrounding landscape. Despite the physical prominence of the sixty-foot sculpture, the sensation is one that the faces seem almost to spontaneously rise from the rock, securing a bond between the sculpture and the material. *Sketched* in a mountain, the visages of the four American presidents lose themselves among the crevices of the mountainous massif from which the figures emerge like silent sentinels. This same interactive relationship between humans and nature is evident also in the archaeological site of Sigiriya, Sri Lanka, which contains the remains of a fifth-century fortress deeply integrated into a spectacular 660-foot massive rock column. The lavish palace, built on the flat summit of this strange hill, was adorned around the massif slopes with hanging gardens, fountains, canals, stairways carved in the rock, and large lions sculpted from stone guarding the entrances. The wonder of this place is captivating: the rocky massif, solitary with its singular conformation in the forest's greenery, seems to shelter the human work within, as in an enormous beehive. Human construction merges seamlessly with rock, autonomously and consciously wondrous. Such is the wonder of the Greek Orthodox monasteries of Meteora in Greece: distant in geography and time from the Fortress in the Sky in Sigiriya, the two architectures share a close relationship between human work and nature's. Daringly constructed on steep walls and

precipitously clinging to the eroding slopes of rock—
to elevations as high as 1,300 feet—the monastery
buildings seem to insert themselves, almost
stealthily, into this landscape unique to the world,
meteora ("suspended in air"), above the lowlands of
Thessaly. Within this autonomous microcosm, the
ascetic communities would have certainly found in
the spectacular landscape a sense of peaceful wonder
mixed with reverential awe.

Quite a different motivation is at the base of
those natural landscapes modified by humans that

unknowingly, spontaneously, create wonder. Born
from purely functional exigence and maintained
for that purpose, certain rural areas, for production
or extraction, recontour the land in geometric
lines and colors that exist midway between the
natural and the artificial. The beautiful salt flats of
Lanzarote, the largest in the Canary Islands, extend
between a gorgeous panoramic promontory and
the beach: the large squared human-created vats
harmonize with the volcanic lagoon overlooking
the sea containing the precious natural mineral.

The silver white salt sparkles a thousand different hues beneath the Lanzarote sun (one of the sunniest islands in Europe), embellishing the natural landscape, a beauty equally enriched in both history and economic wealth, salt the main source of income on the island in recent decades. Drawing attention to the rural landscapes, of undeniable beauty is the Yuanyang rice fields of China, developed on a series of terraces, in which humans have constructed sinuous lines along the height and breadth of the slopes. In particular between February and March, when the 25,000 acres of rice crops are irrigated, water reflects the sun's rays, creating captivating plays of light. On cloudy days or at sunset, the fields are tinged with a thousand colors interwoven by the web of terrace borders. A similar spectacle appears at Batad in the Philippines, where the beauty of the terraces that extend as far as the eye can see adds a geometric harmony, laid out like the plan of an amphitheater, observed from above or at center, an enchanting spectacle not easy to forget.

METEORA MONASTERIES

GREECE

Location: Meteora, Kalambaka, Thessaly, Greece

The monasteries poised on the Meteora possess a timeless charm. From the top of the imposing stone towers that overlook the plains below, the panorama is breathtaking, and the monasteries, hugging the vertiginous cliff slopes seem suspended between worlds, between heaven and earth. Important center of the Greek Orthodox Church, these buildings have found in the unique and unusual morphology of the area, the heart of Thessaly, both a practical and spiritual value. In the fourteenth century, design had to take into account measures of defense against Turkish incursion, but it is clear that the choice of location was also determined by the incredible beauty of the rocky peaks brushing the sky. Elevated above civilization below, concretely and symbolically, the monks created in this inaccessible place an enchanting microcosm, perfect and self-sufficient, in which solitude and silence are master.

OPPOSITE: THE MONASTERY OF ROUSSANOU, PERCHED ON A CLIFF IN METEORA, IS INHABITED BY NUNS.
BELOW: THE SANDSTONE CLIFFS OF METEORA FORM NATURAL TOWERS THAT OVERLOOK THE NORTHWESTERN BORDER OF THE THESSALY PLAIN.
PP. 220-221: THE GREAT METEORON, OR MONASTERY OF THE TRANSFIGURATION OF CHRIST, IS THE LARGEST OF THE MONASTERIES AT METEORA.

Date: XII–XIV century

Definition: Group of monasteries constructed on the summits of towering sandstone cliffs.

Maximum elevation: 1,200 feet.

Descriptive features: The morphology of the land is the result of water and wind erosion of the sandstone. The monasteries were constructed following the settlement in caves by the first hermits and anchorites in the eleventh century; to date, of the twenty-four monasteries, only seven remain intact, and open to visitors.

Acknowledgments: UNESCO World Heritage Site since 1988.

SIGIRIYA, FORTRESS IN THE SKY

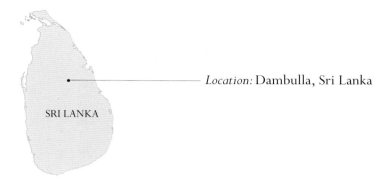

SRI LANKA

Location: Dambulla, Sri Lanka

In a verdant plain, visible from miles away, a tall solitary monolith of volcanic origin emerges with an amazing history. Sigiriya holds the remains of an ancient fortress built in the fifth century by King Kasyapa, which covered nearly 162,000 square feet. Fearing revenge from his brother, whom he had deposed from the throne by force, the king determined to build an impregnable fortress—called the Lion's Fortress—on a spectacular natural formation, consisting of a massive column of rock nearly 660 feet high and surrounded by massive ramparts and moats populated by crocodiles. The residence rises on the summit of the monolith, entered by ascent along a stone stairway, and would have been a complex of extraordinary splendor in its time, with hanging gardens, canals, fountains, statues, bas-reliefs, and frescoes embellishing the interior spaces, the structure itself formed into a labyrinth of corridors, galleries, stairways, as well as many rooms dedicated to the sovereign and his concubines. The gardens in particular would have been breathtaking, lavish symmetrical expanses across the vast space between rock and fortress, terraced gardens along the high rock walls, the work of master landscape architects.

OPPOSITE: THE GATE OF THE LIONS AT THE CITADEL OF SIGIRYA, ONCE DOMINATED BY A LARGE LION'S HEAD. FROM HERE A STONE STAIRWAY LEADS TO THE ROYAL PALACE.
BELOW: DETAIL OF THE BEAUTIFUL FRESCOES OF SIGIRIYA. MOST LIKELY THE PAINTINGS ONCE COVERED A GOOD PART OF THE ROCK FAÇADE, BUT MANY WORKS WERE DESTROYED WHEN THE BUILDING BECAME A MONASTERY, REMOVED SO THEY WOULD NOT DISTRACT FROM MEDITATION.
PP. 224-225: THE MONOLITH THAT HOUSES THE FORTRESS OF SIGIRIYA RISES SUDDENLY IN THE FLAT LANDSCAPE, A SOLITARY AND UNUSUAL TOWER.

Date: V century

Definition: Defensive fortress constructed under King Kasyapa.

Dimensions: Maximum elevation of the hill on which the fortress rises is approximately 660 feet with a sheer drop on both sides.

Descriptive features: The archaeological site of Sigiriya is located on the top of a hill of volcanic origin on which evidence of settlement dates to as early as the Prehistoric Era. Within the fortress walls, the struggle for the throne unfolded between the brothers Kasyapa and Mugalan, ending with the defeat of Mugalan, who threw himself on his sword. Subsequently, the fortress became a monastery, and with this change many of the frescoes were lost, removed by monks who considered them a hindrance to meditation.

Acknowledgments: UNESCO World Heritage Site since 1982.

MOUNT RUSHMORE

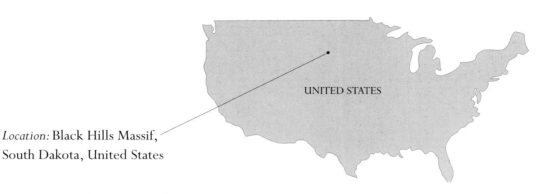

UNITED STATES

Location: Black Hills Massif,
South Dakota, United States

The colossal group portrait of the four presidents carved in the granite of Mount Rushmore seems to emerge naturally from the stone wall of the Black Hills, and, in its grandeur, echoes an ambitious project: to represent the first 150 years of the nation's history across the profiles of a few of the most significant historical figures at salient crossroads of the American story. The intent was as impressive as the construction was demanding: on the sun-exposed side of Mount Rushmore, already part of a national park, about four hundred men and women worked for fourteen years, with 90 percent of the *sculpting* achieved by tons of strategically placed dynamite, which allowed the forms to arrive within three to four inches of their finished characteristics, these final traits completed with a jackhammer. The cultural scope of the work, conceived by the sculptor Gutzon Borglum, engendered a national symbol, and in 1998, to ensure the legacy of American history for future generations, a Hall of Records was carved into the mountain behind the portrait head of Abraham Lincoln, containing the most important documents in American history (US Constitution, Declaration of Independence, Bill of Rights…), sealed behind a giant granite slab. Mount Rushmore is located on land sacred to Native Americans, motivating the construction of a monument, even larger than Mount Rushmore and still under construction after many decades, of the great Lakota chief Crazy Horse.

OPPOSITE AND BELOW: DETAILS OF THE PRESIDENTIAL PORTRAITS ON THE ROCK WALL OF MOUNT RUSHMORE. OPPOSITE, WASHINGTON AND JEFFERSON; BELOW, LINCOLN.

Date: 1941

Definition: Colossal sculpture in granite portraying four presidents of the United States of America (George Washington, Thomas Jefferson, Theodore Roosevelt, and Abraham Lincoln).

Height: 60 feet.

Descriptive features: The sculpture is a symbol of American history, and the monument receives 3 million visitors every year. It has appeared as a focal point in several cinematic works, including Alfred Hitchcock's *International Intrigue* (1959) and *National Treasure: Book of Secrets* (2007).

SALINAS DE JANUBIO

CANARY ISLANDS (SPAIN)

Location: Yaiza, Lanzarote, Canary Islands, Spain

On the lava scarred island of Lanzarote, the linear and colorful landscape and architecture of Janubio's salt pans is striking: some 111 acres of salt vats dedicated to the collection of the precious mineral extend on a lagoon of volcanic origin between a panoramic promontory and the beach overlooking the sea. An important source of income for the island in past decades is today an unforgettable attraction for visitors: the salt expanses stand out for their particular colors, which are only intensified by the copious sunlight, contrasting with the dark blue of the Atlantic. From the blues of the sea salt, characteristic of the Canary Islands, to the intense red of the indigenous crustaceans to the pristine white of Janubio's beach, this corner of Lanzarote is an explosion of color, geometrically partitioned by salt vats, evoking a sort of abstract masterpiece. The aesthetic composition creates an architectural and environmental landscape, founded in history and artisanship, the traditional salt production mechanisms, once fundamental to the economy, still visible on the volcanic terrain.

OPPOSITE, BELOW, AND PP. 230-231:
EVOCATIVE FRAMING OF THE SALT COLLECTION
VATS AT JANUBIO, ENCLOSED BETWEEN SEA
AND HINTERLAND.

Date: 1895—present

Definition: Salt mines constructed on a lagoon of volcanic origin.

Dimensions: Approximately 111 acres.

Descriptive features: The salt flats, for the most part used to preserve fish, produced 10,000 tons of sea salt a year; in recent times, with the introduction of modern systems of refrigeration, production was reduced to one-fifth of its former capacity (roughly 2,000 tons a year). Several explanations are proffered regarding the different colors of the salt: the red seems due to the *artemia*, a small crustacean indigenous to Lanzarote's waters, or particular bacteria in the presence of high salinity. The salt of the lagoon is used to decorate the streets and squares of Arrecife during the celebration of Corpus Christi.

Acknowledgments: The area remains active with the support of the European Union, which has declared it a protected natural area; the island of Lanzarote was designated by UNESCO as a biosphere reserve.

HONGHE HANI RICE TERRACES

CHINA

Location: Yuanyang, Yunnan, China

The Honghe Hani Rice Terraces form a landscape beloved by photographers around the world, where nature has created picturesque rolling hills as far as the eye can see. More than 1,300 years ago, the Hani people sculpted the mountains in curves and spirals, inventing marvelous geometries all in order to harvest most effectively their precious rice, their sustenance. The beauty of the surreal landscape is awe-inspiring, over 25,000 acres of terraces covered in water that reflect both sun and cloud, creating sinuous plays of light and curious reflections against the fog. The effect is intensified by the continuity of the walls that follow one after the other, numbering three thousand vertical terraces from the lowest plain to the tallest terrace. Curiosity is stirred beyond the land itself to the numerous villages clinging to the terraces, where traditional architecture has been preserved and which is still populated by the Hani people, original builders of the irrigation system on the mountain slopes. Still today, harmony presides with the earth, in a timeless landscape.

OPPOSITE, BELOW, AND PP. 234-235: THE RICE TERRACES OF YUANYANG OFFER DIVERSE VIEWS DEPENDING ON THE SEASON, CLIMATE, OR HOUR OF THE DAY.

Date: Constructed in the VIII century AD and active to the present.

Definition: Terraced rice fields built by the indigenous Hani people.

Size: 25,000–33,000 acres.

Descriptive features: The surrounding mountains provide water for irrigation, flowing through a complex system of 4,653 channels, reaching all the fields.

Acknowledgments: UNESCO World Heritage Site since 2013.

PHILIPPINES

BANAUE RICE TERRACES

Location: Banaue, Luzon Island, Philippines

Though thousands of years old, the Banaue rice terraces represent a remarkable example of environmental and *ecological* engineering. Capturing water descending from the mountains and restructuring the slopes (with constructed walls) to the very minimum extent required, the rice terraces have continued their function in the heart of the Philippine Cordilleras, considered by many the eighth wonder of the world and declared by UNESCO a World Heritage Site in 1995. The terraces were constructed by the ancient population of the Ifugao, headhunters, distinguished in their ability and talent to sculpt wood: testament of their craftsmanship can be appreciated in the rice terraces when encountering their representations of the deity Bulol, overseer and protector of the precious rice harvest from adverse weather and predatory animals. The *god of rice* stands vigil over a visual spectacle of intrinsic form, character, and function: an intricate and dense system of ponds bound by stone walls follows the mountain slopes, in a layout resembling a sort of magnificent amphitheater populated with mirrors, where tradition endures the millennia in harmony with nature.

OPPOSITE AND BELOW: THE TERRACES OF BANAUE DEVELOP ON THE SLOPES OF THE PHILIPPINE CORDILLERA, SINUOUSLY OVERLAPPING IN THEIR ASCENT.
PP. 238-239: PANORAMIC VIEW OF THE TERRACES IN THE PROVINCE OF IFUGAO. THE NAME OF THE REGION AND ITS PEOPLE DERIVES FROM *IPUGO*, WHICH MEANS "FROM THE HILL."

Date: Terraces dug approximately 2,000 years ago, still in use.

Definition: Terraced rice fields built by hand on the mountains of the Philippine Cordilleras.

Dimensions: The terraces develop on the slopes up to an altitude of 5,000 feet; the rice fields, if placed side by side in a straight line, would equal more than half the Earth's circumference.

Descriptive features: The terraces were excavated by hand with a few simple tools by the ancestors of the indigenous Ifugao people. The irrigation system is the original ancient construction, drawing water from the rainforests and guiding it through a sequence of stairways, exploiting the slope of the mountain.

Acknowledgments: The Banaue Rice Terraces form part of the Rice Terraces of the Philippine Cordilleras, designated a UNESCO World Heritage Site since 1995.

Copyright © 2015 Sassi Editore Srl
viale Roma 122/b
36015 Schio (VI)
ITALY

© text, Irena Trevisan
© translation, SallyAnn DelVino
© images, as in the photographic credits

This edition published in 2018 by Chartwell Books,
an imprint of The Quarto Group,
142 West 36th Street, 4th Floor,
New York, NY 10018, USA
T (212) 779-4972 F (212) 779-6058
www.QuartoKnows.com

Chartwell Books titles are also available at discount for retail, wholesale, promotional, and bulk purchase. For details, contact the Special Sales Manager by email at specialsales@quarto.com or by mail at The Quarto Group, Attn: Special Sales Manager, 401 Second Avenue North, Suite 310, Minneapolis, MN 55401, USA.

10 9 8 7 6 5 4 3 2 1

ISBN: 978-0-7858-3628-5

For the original Italian edition:
Editor: Luca Sassi
Copyeditor and Designer: Irena Trevisan
Proofreaders: Ester Tomè, Valentina Facci

PHOTOGRAPHIC CREDITS

All photographs are from the © Shutterstock online archive, in particular:

P. 6-7, 52-53: © Hung Chung Chih
P. 50: © lapas77
P. 51: © SIHASAKPRACHUM
P. 54-55: © VLADJ55
P. 57: © Serg Zastavkin
P. 60: © Koraysa
P. 67: © Steve Lovegrove
P. 68-69: © Vadim Petrakov
P. 71: © Sorin Colac
P. 106: © saiko3p
P. 120-121: © Frederic Legrand
P. 133: © ostill
P. 136: © Chris Howey
P. 144: © Photobac
P. 145: © robert paul van beets
P. 223: © Goran Bogicevic

Printed in China / SASSI171221CV